STRUCTURE AND COGNITION
Aspects of Hindu Caste and Ritual

Structure and Cognition

Aspects of Hindu Caste and Ritual

VEENA DAS

SECOND EDITION

DELHI
OXFORD UNIVERSITY PRESS
CALCUTTA   CHENNAI   MUMBAI

Oxford University Press, Walton Street, Oxford OX2 6DP

Oxford   New York
Athens   Auckland   Bangkok   Calcutta
Cape Town   Chennai   Dar es Salaam   Delhi
Florence   Hong Kong   Istanbul   Karachi
Kuala Lumpur   Madrid   Melbourne   Mexico City
Mumbai   Nairobi   Paris   Singapore
Taipei   Tokyo   Toronto

and associates in

Berlin   Ibadan

ISBN 0 19 562651 6

Printed in India
at Rekha Printers Pvt. Ltd., New Delhi 110020
and published by Manzar Khan, Oxford University Press
YMCA Library Building, Jai Singh Road, New Delhi 110001

for Dev

for Dev

Contents

Contents

Preface to the Second Edition

It has been my good fortune that this book is now going into a second edition. This is not, however, an unmixed blessing, for I have been faced with the difficult task of deciding what changes I should make in response to the criticisms made in the various reviews of this book which were invariably thoughtful and fair. In the end, I decided to respond to one major criticism. This related to the difficulty which many reviewers felt in extending the conclusions presented here for a general understanding of myths and rituals in Hindu culture. I have now added an Epilogue which, I hope, will go some way towards meeting this criticism.

Except for minor alterations, the main body of the text remains unchanged. This does not mean that there was not room for substantive revision. It is only that small, piecemeal changes here and there might have met certain criticisms in a technical sense but these would have failed to do justice to the seriousness with which these criticisms were offered. I am particularly unhappy in my description of the king's domain as that of temporal power. I think the text makes it clear that I am referring to the king's exclusion from functions of priesthood, but the relation between kingship and divinity needs to be further explored.

In this book, the texts normally used by Indologists have been appropriated for an anthropological discourse. Clearly, I work with a theory of text which is different from the dominant Indological tradition set by such writers as Kane and Gonda, among others. I expect that this is related to different concerns of anthropologists and Indologists. I have deliberately not followed the style of presentation demanded by textual exegesis in Indology, so as to make the book readily accessible to those who are not trained in Indology, whether their interest lies in popular Hinduism or the cross-cultural study of myth and ritual. It has given me great pleasure that Indologists and historians have found this book of some interest and I can only apologize to them that it departs so radically from the style of textual exegesis established in their disciplines.

In preparing the second edition, I have had the privilege of receiv-

ing comments from many scholars. In particular, I wish to thank
Ralph Nicholas, T. N. Madan, Ronald Inden, McKim Marriott,
Audrey Hayley, S. J. Tambiah, Ashis Nandy, and Imtiaz Ahmad.
My husband and children provided considerable help in their usual
cheerful manner. Such a small book can hardly bear the burden of so
much indebtedness but I hope to utilize the comments offered on this
book in future work.

The Bombay University selected this book for the Ghurye Award
in 1977 and I take this opportunity to express my gratitude for this
honour. Finally, I wish to thank the amiable people at the Oxford
University Press for the mixture of firmness and consideration with
which they handle their authors. Although they must have despaired
at my inability to meet deadlines, I was always treated with courtesy
and kindness.

VEENA DAS

1 August 1981

Preface to the First Edition

THIS study seeks to understand the Hindu theories of caste and ritual from the Hindu texts. It tries to make comprehensible the structure of texts which until recently have been regarded as a peculiar mixture of myth and history. I find it difficult to accept that a text is only a random juxtaposition of ideas simply because the structure within which its author or compiler has conceived it is not our idea of a structure. Hence the cognitive structure of the texts has been presented here in its totality.

I began my research on these themes in 1966 for my Ph.D. dissertation which was completed in 1970 under the supervision of Professor M. N. Srinivas. It was largely his encouragement which made me take up what was a very unorthodox endeavour in sociology in 1966. The development of Hindu 'ethno-sociology' meanwhile encourages one to believe that the Hindus' own view of their society is now going to be treated with some seriousness. I am deeply indebted to Professor Srinivas for many stimulating arguments on this theme and for a dialogue which has continued for ten years.

My colleagues in the Delhi School of Economics have provided lively discussion and debate. I am especially grateful to Professors André Béteille and A. M. Shah for help and critical comments in various stages of writing this book. Professor J. P. S. Uberoi has always shared his ideas with generosity. But for his participation in the evolution of these ideas I am sure the analysis would never have been completed. Whenever I have been unsure, I have inflicted whole chapters on Meena Kaushik and Shiv Visvanathan and they have patiently pointed out contradictions and likely sources of confusion. Most of all, my husband Ranen has been a tremendous source of sustenance, as well as the most consistent critic of my work.

I express my sincere thanks to Mr Ramesh Shroff, Professors U. B. Shah and A. N. Mehta for their help in tracing the texts of the caste Puranas; to Mr and Mrs Imdad Ali for their generous hospitality during my stay in Ahmedabad; to the staff of the Ratan Tata Library for their cooperation; to the Centre of Advanced Study in Sociology for a grant towards the preparation of the manuscript; to the Institute for the Study of Human Issues Inc. and *Contributions to Indian Sociology, n.s.*, for permission to use material in Chapters 4 and 5 respectively from my articles which were originally published in their journals; to Mr R. L. Kalra for typing the manuscript with great care; and to Oxford University Press for their editorial contribution.

VEENA DAS

Delhi
January 1977

Note on Transliteration

SANSKRIT proper names are used in the text in their English version. Sanskrit terms have been *italicized*. Sanskrit proper names and terms have been formally transliterated in Appendix 1.

1

Introduction

THE purpose of this study is to examine Hindu caste and ritual from the point of view of the cultural meanings associated with their institutionalized manifestations. We have chosen to examine the cultural meanings of these through a monographic study of certain selected texts in Sanskrit. We are aware that anthropologists do not normally resort to the study of Sanskrit texts to understand the social institutions of India, but hope that this study will show the importance of using literary texts for the examination of different aspects of Hindu social life.

Since Indologists have always treated the religious texts in Sanskrit as the most important sources of knowledge about Indian society, the departure from this particular point of view in social anthropology has been marked by the insistence of anthropologists that empirical fieldwork tradition is necessary for a proper understanding of Indian society. For instance, Srinivas, who is strongly associated with the fieldwork tradition of social anthropology in India, thinks that to understand any aspect of Indian society through a study of Sanskrit texts is fraught with many risks (Srinivas, 1962b). He emphasizes that the book-view of Indian society is only a 'sectional' view of social reality and it vitiates actual observation of social behaviour. In a similar vein Bailey has forcefully expressed himself against the view that Indian sociology should be defined to include Indological materials (Bailey, 1964). This shift from the approach considered typical of Indologists to the approach considered typical of social anthropologists has certainly helped to build up knowledge about the functioning of social institutions, based upon first-hand information acquired in the field through participant observation.

From another point of view, however, the central place accorded to observation in anthropological research and the development of a positivist approach has had certain undesirable consequences as it has been accompanied by a studied refusal to discuss the epistemological issues about the basis of knowledge and the nature of truth. It has often been assumed implicitly by anthropologists that the basis of true knowledge is experience gained through direct confrontation between reality as it was conceived and reality as it exists or between consciousness and being. The epistemological issues involved in this position have been consistently ignored and particularly the problem that to think is to think conceptually. In other words, what is considered to be the objective, existing reality described in anthropological literature has already passed through the filters of prior perception since the anthropologist has antecedent ideas about the relevance of the diversities of facts that he encounters in the field. The relative neglect of these problems has led to the conception of the external world in anthropological writings, as a pre-existing model. Progress in knowledge has been related to the development of a conceptual apparatus which is similar to reality in that it is considered capable of imitating the properties and relations of the external world. The external world is itself seen as independent of this effort and it exists regardless of the success and failure of human knowledge to imitate it. While anthropologists have been right in rejecting the philosophical position that knowledge can be derived from consciousness, the conception of social reality that we have underlined above has invested it with a kind of concreteness that it cannot really possess.

One of the consequences of defining social reality in terms of concreteness has been that the emphasis in anthropological research has shifted from the study of *ideas* to observable *behaviour*. This is because it has often been assumed implicitly that while the way people act can be observed, the way they think cannot be observed. The latter has been assumed to lack concreteness and has therefore not been considered as the proper subject-matter of anthropological research. For example, in the field of religion, ritual behaviour was studied, but not religious thought. In the field of family, emphasis has gradually come to be placed on the size and frequencies of households since these can be observed and counted, to the exclusion of family about which people have nebulous and often contradictory ideas. In the village studies which accumulated in the fifties, one finds descriptions about ownership of land, about exchange of foods and services, but no information about the structure of ideas, about Brahmanhood or untouchability. Yet the emphasis on those aspects of social reality which can be observed directly has clear disadvantages. Households may be easier to count but it is the family which is of central concern to people. The fact that it is not possible to get direct and unambiguous answers on religious thought, does not reduce its importance for anthropological research. It is the very ambiguity and flexibility of the categories of family or the categories used in religious thought which makes them important—both as categories of thought and tools of action. The ambiguities of most important social categories are related to the fact that social life, as Durkheim emphasized, is neither given nor assumed, but is a creation of the human mind.

It would be an exaggeration to say that the conception of truth in anthropological research which we have emphasized above, has invested social reality with the same degree of concreteness for all social anthropologists of India. There has been an important difference between those anthropologists who prefer to define away all ambiguities and concentrate only on that which can be unambiguously replicated at the conceptual level and those anthropologists who have considered ambiguities to be central to social life. An example of the former is the recent work of Shah (1973) on the household in a Gujarat village, where his descriptions are limited to the frequencies and compositions of household since this is the clearest and least vague. On the other hand, the works of Srinivas show his sensitivity to the ambiguities in social life and the uses to which these are put. However, even Srinivas does not go beyond replicating these ambiguities at the conceptual level, and the identity of a phenomenon which may lie behind the many concrete manifestations is not analysed. I believe that this position derives from the particular conception of truth to which he adheres.

An important departure is found in the writings of Louis Dumont, who not only rejects the dichotomy between thought and behaviour but also insists that an explanatory model cannot be limited to a replication of observed reality. This is why he tries to reduce observed diversities of thought and behaviour to certain basic structural patterns, of which the actors may not themselves be aware, but which lie behind manifest diversities. Thus, one important difference between the structural method which Dumont applies to Indian society and the earlier methods is in their conceptualization of the relation between knowledge and social reality. Whether one agrees with the substantive parts of Dumont's writings or not, the altered conception of the nature of anthropological explanation itself constitutes a landmark in Indian sociology.

Dumont's method is important because it seems likely that in the near future considerable emphasis will be placed on studying how people organize their material world. The 'ethno-sociology' propagated by McKim Marriott and the application of cultural analysis, first developed by Schneider (1968) for the study of American kinship, to Bengali kinship by Inden and Nicholas (1977) point to a direction in which more anthropologists will be concerned with delineating the principles of classification used by the people themselves. This shift from a study of facts which are observable by the anthropologist to people's ideas about the systems in which they operate is important. However, it is still not very clear whether the principal aim of cultural analysis is simply to present the native ordering of the material world, or whether its proponents intend to construct explanatory models which would have as their subject matter the type of orderliness which people impose on the world in which they live. Nicholas and Inden come close to the first position. In this case the conception of truth does not seem to have altered, since it still consists of the replication of a pre-existing reality. The only difference, and this is not to deny that it is an important one, is that 'pre-existing reality' is now defined to include primarily systems of thought. It seems to us that the basic issue to which ethno-sociology must discover an answer is the epistemological one of the relation between knowledge and reality in their models.

For the moment, then, if we accept the position that the way in which people impose order upon the world is important as a subject of study for anthropological research, and that the models one constructs for understanding this order need not be replications of the native order itself, the question immediately arises as to how the study of such materials is to be made feasible. Two kinds of answers suggest themselves. First of all, one can collect information about cognitive systems through fieldwork, as has been done by the followers of the componential school as well as the proponents of cultural analysis. Secondly, one can take the finished products of collective consciousness such as the corpus of myths and extract the principles underlying the conceptual orders envisaged in these myths. Such exercises have become part of anthropological tradition after the classic writings of Lévi-Strauss.

Since India has had a long and continuous literate tradition it becomes necessary to distinguish between the literate and oral traditions in the sociology of India though the two are by no means unrelated. However, since the large masses of India are illiterate, some anthropologists have been of the view that social anthropology in India should be limited to the study of multiplex relations to be found in the relatively self-sufficient villages or tribes in India. The strongest proponent of this view is Bailey (1964). To limit the scope of anthropology in this manner, however, amounts to treating a literate civilization as a non-literate primitive society. This can be as one-sided as the assumption that all knowledge about Indian society can be derived from the study of Sanskrit texts. Indeed, what impresses one in the writings of the early pioneers of Indian sociology is the sense of richness, complexity and sophistication of Indian civilization that they are able to convey.

But to come back to those anthropologists who have reacted against the Indologist's endeavour to derive all knowledge of India from the study of Sanskrit texts, one cannot fail to notice that this reaction led to a redefinition of certain subjects of study like Hinduism. The Indologists often assumed, for instance, that 'true' Hinduism was to be found in descriptions in the Sanskrit texts and that the religious customs practised by the large majority of peasants were 'superstitions'. It was Srinivas (1952) who insisted that the religion of the peasant was as integral a part of Hinduism as the scriptures. His distinction between Sanskritic and non-Sanskritic Hinduism stressed the fact that Hinduism also existed outside the Sanskritic texts. However, in posing this dichotomy Srinivas failed to see that, while Sanskritic Hinduism may not be replicated at the non-Sanskritic level, there was a possibility that both worked with common structural categories so that the religion of the illiterate peasant might constitute a structural transformation of the religion of the sophisticated literati.

It would follow that anthropologists cannot afford to leave the study of Sanskrit texts to Indologists alone. Dumont's contention that one must give due emphasis to the study of Indological materials in order to discover the constants of the Indian civilization should be strongly supported (Dumont, 1957). However Dumont, like his predecessors Mauss and Dumézil from the French school and Ghurye, Coomaraswamy, Kapadia and Karve among the Indian sociologists, has used Indological materials in piecemeal fashion, usually for purposes of illustration. The built-in bias for the author's own conclusions in this procedure is obvious. It therefore seems necessary to develop an approach for the study of Sanskrit texts in a monographic framework instead of using them merely for purposes of illustration. This approach would make it possible to analyse the structure of a text in its entirety.

In the present study two texts in Sanskrit, dealing with different types of themes, have been selected for detailed analysis. The first is the Dharmaranya Purana, a mythical history of the Modh Brahmans and Modh Baniyas of Gujarat. The second is the Grihya Sutra of Gobhila, which provides the earliest detailed instructions for the performance of what are known as domestic rites.

Our choice of a text which deals primarily with the history of a caste was guided by an interest in understanding how the different caste categories are conceptualized in Hindu thought. It is often assumed, for instance, that the term Brahman refers to a particular *jati* empirically observed. However, in addition to being a category which describes a particular empirically observed group, the term 'Brahman' is also a conceptual category of Hindu thought. With a few notable exceptions such as Dumont, anthropologists are relatively silent on the meanings associated with Brahmanhood in Hindu thought. Indologists, on the other hand, have often pointed out the varied contexts in which the term Brahman is applied. In order to understand the identity behind the many usages of the term it is necessary to move from an internal definition of the concept in terms of its intrinsic properties to an external definition in terms of its relations with other concepts which make up the complete universe of discourse. As Boudon (1972) has argued, the shift from an internal definition of a concept to an external one has constituted a major breakthrough in varied subjects from epistemology to structural linguistics. He illustrates this argument with an example in which the changing definitions about the concept of axiom are described. In his words,

The same is true of the concept of *axiom*. It is not long since efforts were made to define these concepts from their synonyms, *untestability*, *prior*, *given*, etc., though the commonplace stating that a deductive argument necessarily supposed a body of unproven propositions was acknowledged in the end. Of course an *axiom*, defined in terms of its intrinsic properties, is an unproven proposition. Therefore it was thought for centuries that certain propositions must be the starting point of an argument *because* they were untestable or *intuitively* true. The epistemological difficulties raised by the concept of axiom did not vanish until it was understood that an axiom was not a proposition placed at the beginning of a deductive argument because it was untestable—but rather a proposition made untestable by its location at the beginning of an argument. This realization surmounted the difficulties arising from the concepts of test and falsification, as well as the contradiction due to the fact that that the same proposition can be stated as an axiom in one context and a demonstratable hypothesis in another. [Boudon, 1971:9–10]

It is true that Dumont has made a major breakthrough in analysing the meanings of the conceptual categories of sanyasa (renunciation), kingship, and Brahmanhood, not on the basis of the intrinsic properties of each but on the basis of their relations to each other. However, as we hope to show later, Dumont has been guilty of what was called the distortion of a semantic field by Lévi-Strauss (1963) in a different context. The universe of discourse has been incorrectly specified by him. In our analysis of the Dharmaranya Purana, we find that it is not possible to discuss kingship only in relation to Brahmanhood, or renunciation only in relation to the man-in-the-world, as Dumont has done. It is the interrelationship of all these categories which defines the universe of discourse, and selecting pairs of binary relations, one at a time, amounts to a misstatement of the problem. As the analysis in the next chapter will show, the empirical categories Brahman, Vanika, king, and sanyasi have been used as conceptual tools in the text to express the structural order of Hinduism. Towards this end, the statements about these empirical categories have been first interconnected as propositions in formal logic. These logical relations have been used to formulate abstract ideas about the statuses Brahmanhood, householdership, kingship, and ascetism. At the next level the statuses have been interconnected in terms of logical relations of opposition, exclusion, and exchange. These relations between the statuses express the structural order of Sanskritic Hinduism in terms of a mediated opposition between the asocial and social, and within the social in terms of a categorical partition between the holders of temporal power (king), inherent spiritual merit (Brahman), and the non-Brahman mass of householders within the caste system.

It is obvious that the model of Sanskritic Hinduism that we have constructed does not lie at the surface of the text. In fact, in the text one only comes across various stories in which Brahmans, kings, Vanikas, and sanyasis appear in various forms in different contexts. However, though the structure that we have extracted may not lie at its surface, it helps us to find out the identity of meaning behind the various uses of these categories found in the text. Since we do not expect the model of Sanskritic Hinduism to be a replication of the reality conceived at the surface level in the text, the test of its validity lies in its logical coherence and the economy of explanation which it helps us to achieve. Most importantly, it is a demonstration of our statement that the meaning of Brahmanhood, kingship, and ascetism in Hindu thought cannot be extracted from the intrinsic properties of these categories but lies in their relations to each other.

Moving away from myths to ritual, the Hindu theory makes a distinction between domestic rituals and public rituals. The former include such rituals as performed on the occasion of birth, initiation, marriage, and for the propitiation of ancestors. The latter include the ritualization of public events such as coronations, commemorations of victory, propitiation of gods through *soma* sacrifices, etc. It is significant that in the Hindu scheme, the rituals performed at death are not included in the category of domestic rituals.[1] Indeed, the Hindu scheme does not consider death to be an event primarily involving the domestic group. This is shown by the fact that ideally a Hindu should not die in his house but on the *ghats* of a sacred river (cf. *Krityakalpataru*). Even today one can find a large number of people in the pilgrim centres such as Kashi, Mathura, Vrindavan, and Hardwar who have come there with the intention of 'getting release from their mortal bodies'. As Hsu (1964) has noted much earlier, whereas the Chinese prefer to bury their dead in their own compounds, the cremation of a Hindu in all castes takes place on a sacred *ghat*, on the banks of a river or another source of water. Consistent with this is the position which we have developed later, that death rituals do not form an integral part of domestic rituals.

Having completed the analysis of the Dharmaranya Purana which gave the Sanskritic conception of the category of caste and its relations with other categories, we wished to analyse the conception of a domestic group in Sanskritic lore. Since domestic groups do not have a corporate character it was obviously not possible to find 'histories' of domestic groups. But since the domestic group provides the central category for a whole class of rituals we decided to analyse one of the manuals of rituals, known as the Grihya Sutras. On examining the extant Grihya Sutras, the differences were found to be very marginal. The major difference is between those authors who begin the manual with marriage rites and those who begin it with initiation

[1] For an elaboration of this point, see Chapter 4.

rites. We finally selected the Grihya Sutra of Gobhila for detailed analysis because this is considered to be the most complete of the extant texts on Grihya rituals. (See Macdonell, 1899.)

As described earlier, the categories of caste in addition to those of kingship and renunciation provide the conceptual tools for describing the structural order of Hinduism in the Dharmaranya Purana. In contrast, it is ideas of fertility, prosperity, life and death which are sought to be ritualized in the Grihya Sutras and spatial categories provide the conceptual tools for expressing these ideas. Further, in association with the symbolism of laterality, the cardinal points provide symbols for representing different types of movements in the Grihya Sutras. The most important of these is the ritualization of the passage of time, transition from one social status to another, especially as it relates to the structure of the domestic group, and representation of death as a passage from the status of the living human being to that of an ancestor. Incidentally, rituals for the propitiation of ancestors figure in a major way in the Grihya Sutras. Thus, one of the important differences between caste Puranas and Grihya Sutras is that the former deal with the conceptualization of a problem which is unique to Hindu society, viz. the position of a particular caste within the structural order of medieval Hinduism. In the Grihya Sutras, on the other hand, problems of a more general and universal nature are found. These include the conversion of the natural forces of fertility into the social events of marriage and childbirth, as well as the provision of an intellectual mediation to the phenomenon of death which religious thought everywhere refuses to accept as a terminal event.

Perhaps, consistent with the difference between these two types of conceptual problems is the fact that the Dharmaranya Purana selects culture-specific categories such as Brahman and *sanyasi* as its conceptual tools, while the Grihya Sutra takes the natural categories of the points of the compass to describe the structure of ritual processes. Some recent evidence shows that the use of spatial categories is by no means limited to the Grihya Sutras. Beck (1976) has shown, for instance, that the Hindu use of space is intimately linked with the conceptualization of cosmic forces and the basic structure of the human body. According to her, the former provides the external and encompassing milieu within which the body needs to be properly oriented in terms of space. Thus it seems likely that important points of consistency may emerge in the meanings of the different spatial categories in varied fields such as ritual, architecture, folk-theatre, and the conceptualization of cosmic forces as well as bodily processes.

It is also interesting to note that the symbolic use of the human body in the Grihya Sutra for the conceptualization of certain basic relations is significantly different from its symbolic use in the well-known Purusha Sukta myths relating to the origin of the *varna* system. In the Purusha Sukta, the body is divided into four different parts—the head, the arms, the trunk, and the legs. Each of the *varnas* is said to have emanated from a different part of the body of Purusha. Though the four parts together make up a whole they are not symmetrical to each other. In the Grihya Sutra, it is the symbols of laterality which dominate; the right side of the body is used for the performance of rituals that are associated with life-processes such as marriage and childbirth. On the other hand, in the rituals performed for the propitiation of ancestors it is the left side which dominates. Thus, here again the body has been divided up into two parts but the two parts are inverse and symmetrical, constituting binary opposites.

Before going on to detailed discussions of the two texts that have been selected for analysis, it may be useful to give general information on the caste Puranas as well as the Grihya Sutras. We now turn to a description of these two classes of texts.

The Caste Puranas

The Puranas are defined by Indologists as a class of Sanskrit literature that deals with the five themes of creation, re-creation, genealogies, Manu-cycles of time, and histories of dynasties. The total Puranic literature is divided into two sub-classes—(i) the Maha-Puranas that are eighteen in number and are supposed to deal exclusively with the five themes mentioned above, and (ii) the Upa-Puranas, which are also eighteen in number, are written in the same style as the Maha-Puranas but deal directly with local cults and sects. Historians are of the opinion that these texts are likely to have been compiled between the fifth and seventh centuries A.D. Besides these thirty-six texts there are a large number of texts written in the comparatively recent past (A.D. 1200–1700) which also claim to be Puranas, and sometimes have the same title as a Maha-Purana or an Upa-Purana. This claim is not recognized in classical Indological literature since these texts do not deal with the five themes which are considered typical to the Puranas. In this category may be included the Puranas of particular castes, sects or localities. There is reason to believe that such texts are available for various regions such as Gujarat (Dave, 1962; Das, 1970; Sandesara & Mehta, 1964; Shah & Shroff, 1959), Maharashtra (Carter, 1975), Tamilnadu (Raghavan, 1960) and Bengal (Chakravarti, 1965).

In Gujarat, it is only the Brahmin and Baniya castes which have the tradition of having their histories recorded in the form of a Purana. The Rajputs and other similar castes do not have Puranas. They usually employ Barots, a caste of genealogists, for recording the histories of their lineages, as well as detailed genealogies (Shah & Shroff, 1959). We were able to find mention of thirteen principal Puranas in the literature in Gujarati journals. With the exception of the Coppersmiths, Barbers, and a caste of Wrestlers—all the other Puranas purport to record histories of Brahman or Baniya castes. It therefore becomes necessary at this point to consider some of the principal features of Brahman and Baniya castes which are special to Gujarat.

Though a comprehensive study of the caste system of Gujarat at the regional level has not been made, one of the most notable features of the caste system at this level is the proliferation of small, endogamous castes within the Brahman and Baniya divisions. Kavi Dalpatram in his *Jnatinibandha* (1887) enumerated eighty-four castes in the Brahman division, and the same number of castes in the Baniya division. Secondly, there seems to be a close association between caste-name and the name of a locality. Thus Shrimali Brahmans are those Brahmans who come from Shrimal (modern Bhinmal), Modh Brahmans are those who come from Modhera, Nagar Brahmans come from Vadnagar, and so on. Further subdivisions within a caste such as Nagar are again associated with different localities. Thus, the two major subdivisions among the Nagar Brahmans are the Vadnagar Brahmans and the Visalnagar Brahmans—the former's place of domicile is supposed to be the town Vadnagar and the latter's Visalnagar.

A similar association between locality and caste name is found among the castes of the Baniya division also. Thus we get the unique situation in which the same locality provides the point of reference for persons of both Brahman and Baniya castes. Thus Modhera is the town after which both the Modh Brahmans and the Modh Baniyas are named. Similarly Nagar Brahmans and Nagar Baniyas derive their name from Vadnagar. This segmentation of caste along lines of locality which runs parallel for both the Brahman and the Baniya castes is a unique feature of the caste system of Gujarat. The author of the Imperial Gazetteer of Bombay noted that the proliferation of the Brahman and Baniya castes on the basis of territory in Gujarat was unparalleled elsewhere. There are some castes among Brahmans such as the Anavil Brahmans who have no counterpart among the Baniyas and vice versa but these cases are very few.

It will be seen from the above discussion that the Brahman and Baniya castes have important urbanized segments within the region. It would be difficult, in contrast, to find such associations with an urban centre for peasant castes such as Patidars or Kanbis. It is also interesting to note that the Rajputs who do not have the tradition of having caste Puranas have an elaborate system for recording genealogies which is consistent with the elaborate system of lineage organization within that caste. The Brahmans and Baniyas, compared to the Rajputs, are smaller castes and the internal segmentation within the caste is on lines of locality rather than lineage. In fact, in a recent paper Shah (1976) has noted that even when Brahmans and Baniyas own land they do not show any tendency to form lineages. The internally undifferentiated character of these castes is consistent with the identification of the whole caste with a single Purana.

The caste Puranas of Gujarat were written between the twelfth and seventeenth centuries A.D. Internal evidence from the Puranas as well as supporting archaeological evidence has proved beyond reasonable doubt that the texts could not have been written earlier (cf. Dave, 1962; Mehta, n.d.). It is interesting to note that this is the period of the rise and establishment of the Muslim power in Gujarat. But before the establishment of the Muslim power, Gujarat was a region which had been opened to overseas trade and hence had developed important port towns. As a result the mercantile communities, i.e. the Baniyas, occupied an important position in the caste structure of Gujarat. Since heterodox sects such as Jains had their primary following among the mercantile communities, the conflict between the propagation of the Jain faith and the Brahmans was very sharp in Gujarat.[1] These facts are reflected in the caste Puranas. For instance, the Dharmaranya Purana mentions Alauddin (Khilji) by name and describes the battle between the Muslim army and the army of Raja Karna in which the latter was defeated. Similarly, most of the Puranas contain stories about learned debates between the

[1] For a detailed discussion of these points, see Thapar (1972).

Jain monks and Brahmans. Social historians could perhaps explore why there was such a spurt in the production of mythical histories in Sanskrit for these urbanized Brahman and Baniya castes in a period when Muslim culture was becoming predominant in the urban centres of Gujarat. Similarly, the precise dimensions of the relation between kingship, sect, and caste in medieval Hinduism can be examined with the help of these texts.

Certain themes seem to recur in most caste Puranas. These relate to the creation or establishment of Brahmans to commemorate the sacredness of a place, the creation of Vanikas to manage the property of the Brahmans, and acceptance of gifts from the king by Brahmans after initial hesitation and their consequent loss of certain powers. While we have adopted a monographic framework for analysis of the Dharmaranaya Purana, the themes occurring in it are not atypical and are also found in other caste Puranas.

It may be relevant here to give an indication of the social contexts in which the caste Puranas were used. We have discussed this question in detail elsewhere (Das, 1968). Here it is only necessary to recapitulate the main arguments.

Indologists and social historians alike have used texts of this kind for purposes of historical reconstruction. Thus Sandesara and Mehta in their preface to the Mallapurana observe that 'some historical material is occasionally seen, through the mesh of semi-religious and semi-fictitious accounts of the origin of the castes' (Sandesara & Mehta, 1964: 1). Their main endeavour is to sift the genuine historical material from the mythical material. While this approach may have some utility, it is much more profitable to try and explain the structure of these texts in their entirety. To see confused history in these texts is to misinterpret the *rationale* of the documents which has to be established before one can make a proper assessment of these texts. After all, the authors of these texts were not necessarily interested in providing an objective history of the group. In support of this argument an example may be given here. Historians have recently become interested in examining the patterns of Brahman settlements in the different regions of India (see, for example, Kesavan, 1974a, 1974b). They have used various sources of evidence, including texts in Sanskrit. Some of these texts have stories of Brahmans migrating to their present homes from certain towns in the North—e.g. Kanauj, Bareilly, and others. Historians accept this as valid material for historical reconstruction and use it as evidence of the Aryan migration from the north to different parts in southern and eastern India. However, it is equally plausible that the texts may have been written by upwardly mobile local groups in these places who wished to establish their bona fides as Brahmans. In the latter case the stories about migration may be profitably used by historians to explore the people's ideas about sacred geography but not as actual records of Brahman migration. Unfortunately, an assessment of the texts in terms of the social milieu in which they were written and the purpose they served is hardly ever made.

There must have been different kinds of motives that lay behind the tradition of having the history of castes recorded in the form of a Purana. It is quite likely that in the period of rising Muslim power, the Brahman and Baniya groups felt it necessary to have such texts which should affirm their separate identity. The texts themselves do not provide any information about authorship or the contexts in which these were used. However, there is one important exception to this which needs to be considered in some detail. The Devanga Purana, which recounts the legendary origin and history of the Tamil weavers community, has a preface which describes the exact context in which the Purana was used by the caste (Raghavan, 1960).

The preface relates that the weavers of Bodinayakanur (a small town near Coimbatore–Erode) wished to be considered for a higher caste rank. They took their case to the zamindar of Bodinayakanur who then commissioned three Tamil scholars—Sadashivaswami of Coimbatore, Daddaya Deshakar of Kallapadi and Nanahalar Kavichange Navalar of Palana—to give a Tamil rendering of the original version of the Devanga Purana which was in Sanskrit. The translation of the Sanskrit version was made in verse and a prose gloss was added. This was then revised by a certain Sadashiva Iyer who was the guru (spiritual preceptor) of the weaver caste. After that the text was submitted to the zamindar for his decision.

Thus it seems that one of the important social contexts in which a caste could be called upon to submit their Purana was in the courts of kings or important political heads, who were vested with the power to settle disputes relating to rank, privileges, or disabilities of the castes within their respective jurisdictions. It would be futile to expect that the caste Puranas provide an objective record of the history of the caste for this purpose. Clearly, the caste Puranas would have to provide evidence of the caste group's claim to a particular status. However, the 'evidence' itself would have to conform to the canons of legitimacy as defined by the texts of Sanskritic learning. This is why even when the history of one particular *jati* was being presented, the authors did not begin by placing that particular *jati* in relation to other like *jatis*. Instead, they first established the conceptual order of Hinduism by the use of categories taken from the *varna* scheme and the *ashrama* scheme, and only then proceeded to discuss the position of the caste within this order.

From what we have said above, it should not be inferred that the only context in which particular caste groups used their Puranas was in the courts of political authorities, for purposes of establishing a particular claim. The Brahman groups whose position in the caste system was well-established also had caste Puranas. For instance, the Nagar Brahmans who were considered very high in the caste hierarchy in the medieval period in Gujarat also have the Nagar Khanda, a lengthy text which gives their mythical history. Thus the Puranas were group documents which expressed the caste group's perception of itself. Sometimes a mobile group might also express its aspirations through the caste Purana. Similarly, the Puranas of sects and localities expressed the identity of sectarian and local groups. These documents provide very important sources for reconstructing the structure of medieval Hinduism, but it is not legitimate to use them as sources for descriptions of actual events.

In fact, what Lévi-Strauss said of myths can be said about these texts also. According to him,

... it is always rash to undertake, as Boas wanted to do in his monumental *Tsimshian Mythology*, 'a description of the life, social organization, and religious ideas and practices of a people ... as it appears from their mythology ...'
The myth is certainly related to given [empirical] facts, but not as a *representation* of them. The relationship is of a dialectic kind, and the myths can be the opposite of the real institutions. This will in fact always be the case when the myth is trying to express a negative truth. [Lévi-Strauss, 1968: 29]

In the case of the story of Asdiwal he showed how a matrilineal-virilocal people 'discuss' the contradictions which would arise out of a combination of matrilineal descent and uxorilocal residence through the story of Asdiwal. This is the meaning of the statement that the relation between myth and real institutions is a dialectic one and that myths may be used to express a negative truth. However, while one is in agreement with Lévi-Strauss's warnings against the use of myths as representations of empirical facts, the mode of argument in a myth is not always dialectical. The mythical reality is a transformation of observed reality, but it is precisely the alchemy which needs to be investigated. The procedure we have used is to abstract the design-plan of each myth by restating the sequence of incidents in the myth in a contracted form, in a new arrangement. This design-plan then makes the latent patterns of the myth visible and leads to a decoding of the myth (cf. Stanner, 1963). It is to be hoped that the analysis may be of interest not only to sociologists but also to historians.

Of the available caste Puranas, we have selected the Dharmaranya Purana for detailed analysis. As stated earlier, the Dharmaranya Purana purports to recount the 'history' of the Modh Brahmans and Baniyas. The Modh Brahmans, though a subcaste of the Brahmans, do not seem to have occupied a very prestigious position among the Brahmans. For instance, it is recorded that the Modh Brahmans used to accept bride-wealth for their daughters—a custom which is usually associated with low-ranking castes (van der Veen, 1972). The Dharmaranya Purana of the Modh Brahmans and Baniyas bears the same name as one of the Maha-Puranas though the contents of the two texts are entirely different. Incidentally, this is also true of the Vayu Purana which is the caste Purana of the Vayad Brahmans and Baniyas since this text too bears no relation to the well-known Maha-Purana of the same name. The Dharmaranya Purana was probably written sometime between the fourteenth and and fifteenth centuries A.D. It mentions Alauddin by name and castigates Madhava, a minister of Raja Karna, for betraying the king. Since Raja Karna was defeated and expelled in 1303–4 from his capital Patan by the army of Alauddin, this dating of the Purana seems reasonable. In addition, internal linguistic evidence also points to this probable date. (See Misra, 1962).

This text was chosen because it is available in a complete form, whereas Puranas of the Anavils, Vayads, Shrimali Brahmans and Baniyas have been published only in the form of selections. The entire text of the Nagar Khanda is also available but its length (278 chapters) has made historians feel that it was compiled at different periods by different sets of people (Mehta, n.d.). For these reasons, it was considered safer to begin our endeavour by concentrating on the Dharmaranya Purana.

The Grihya Sutras belong to *sutra* literature, and are thought to have been compiled between *c.* 500–200 B.C. (Macdonell, 1899). Along with the Shrauta Sutras, they are manuals of sacrificial ritual. The Shrauta Sutras, fourteen in number, deal with very complicated sacrifices. These are two main groups of sacrifices described in the Shrauta texts: *havi* (oblation) sacrifice, and *soma* sacrifices. The latter were very elaborate, even the simplest requiring sixteen officiating priests. The sacrifices described in the Shrauta Sutras were not congregational, but were offered on behalf of an individual (*yajamana*). The Shrauta Sutras assume the Brahmanic literature, and these texts can be seen as a continuation of the ritual side of Brahmanical literature.

In contrast to the Shrauta rituals, the Grihya rituals did not find any description in Brahmanical literature. Therefore, the compilers of these texts had to rely on the popular tradition, which perhaps accounts for their simplicity. The principal Grihya Sutras are those of Sankhayana, Sambavya, Asvalayana, Gobhila, Paraskara, Apastamba and Kaushika. The details of the ceremonies described in these texts is given in Chapter 4, and detailed descriptions of these texts are available in most standard histories of Sanskrit literature.

2

On the Categories
Brahman, King and Sanyasi

THIS and the following chapter analyse the Dharmaranya Purana. In the present chapter those myths are analysed which relate to the meaning of the categories Brahman, king, and *sanyasi*, and show that the conceptual order of Hinduism is presented in the myths through a categorical partition of these three categories. We shall present the relevant myths in the first section and then proceed to their analysis in the subsequent sections. It may be noted in passing that the following myths have been condensed from several chapters in the Purana. In the usual Puranic style the myths are related either in the form of a conversation between the mythical figures, Yudhishthira and Dhaumya, or presented by the *sutradhar* —a figure who usually introduces a story or a drama in Sanskrit literature.

I

MYTH (1): *The Creation of Dharmaranya*

This myth relates the way in which the place of pilgrimage, Dharmaranya, was created. It is told in the form of a dialogue between Dhaumya and Yudhishthira. Dhaumya first recounts the destruction and creation of the world, and then relates how 'Dharmaranya was created' in the new cycle of time. The story of the creation of the world goes as follows:

At the end of one cycle of time, Shiva in his Rudra form destroyed all living beings. The five elements—earth, fire, water, air, and sky—entered Vishnu and only the primeval being (*adipurusha*) was left. Then the primeval being saw the void and first created water. In the water he threw semen and from the resultant foam the sun was created. From the sun came the air, from air the fire, from fire Omkara (the sacred sound Om) and from Omkara came the seven worlds. Then Gayatri (a sacred verse) was born and from her came Sarasvati (the goddess of learning). From Sarasvati the four Vedas were born and from the Vedas the Puranas were born.

After this there is a break in the story and Yudhishthira asks Dhaumya to relate the story of the creation of the world in greater detail. Then Dhaumya tells the story of how Dharmaranya, the best place of pilgrimage, comparable to the Brahman who is the best of *varnas* and *sanyasa* which is the best of *ashramas*, was created. According to Dhaumya's narration, after Brahma the creator had finished creating everything, Vishnu was pleased with him and offered him a boon. Brahma said: 'If you are pleased with me, then please make this place pure and good enough for gods to reside in. Please establish Brahmans here.'

Vishnu granted this boon and called Rudra. Together the three gods meditated on the three Vedas and thus from the mouth of each god were created six thousand Brahmans who were learned in the Vedas. After this Vishnu asked Vishvakarma, the celestial architect, to build a beautiful and pure city there. At the completion of the city, the gods gave villages, pure land, and fields full of crops to the Brahmans for their livelihood and settled them in the city. Dhaumya ends this story by saying: ' . . . thus the way the greatest of *tirthas* [place of pilgrimage] was created has been described by me.'

MYTH (2): *The Creation of Vanikas*

This myth is the story of the creation of Vanikas as narrated by Dhaumya to Yudhishthira.

Of the Brahmans that were created in Dharmaranya by the three gods, some meditated, others performed *yajna* (holy sacrifices to fire), some performed *yoga*, some spent their time in acts of devotion to God, and others were busy in thinking about political ethics (*rajniti*). Thus they had no time for household affairs. In order to resolve this difficulty, they meditated on the gods who appeared before them. Then they told the gods that they were too busy to manage their household affairs. Besides, they said household affairs awaken desire and greed, and once greed is awakened, where is knowledge and where is happiness?

On hearing this from the Brahmans, the gods were pleased and they thought of Kamadhenu, the celestial cow who grants all desires.

When the cow appeared, Brahma asked her to create thirty-six thousand Vanikas who should be good at household affairs, ready to serve, religious and devoted to Vishnu, who would serve the Brahmans.

To fulfil the god's command, Kamadhenu kicked the earth with the front part of her front hooves and from this earth arose thirty-six thousand Vanikas who were ready to serve, had the *shikha* (hair-knot) and the sacred thread, and were inclined towards giving charity.

They bowed to the gods and asked Vishnu the reason why they had been created, what their duty would be and how they were to earn their living. They further inquired about their name and their *gotras*, and wondered how their *vansha* (lineage) would increase since there were no women of their *varna*.

Brahma said, 'Since you were created by the front hooves of a cow, you will be known as Gobhuja ['cow limb']. You should serve the Brahmans, should be devoted to Vishnu and should be adept in household work.'

In order to get wives for the Vanikas, Brahma thought of Vishvavasu Gandharva. When the Gandharva appeared, Brahma told him that the celestial cow had created the Shudras who were to be known as Gobhujas. He requested the Gandharva to give them wives who should have good fortune, should be religious, and should serve the Brahmans. Vishvavasu Gandharva created girls with celestial beauty, who were married off to the Vanikas so that they could fulfil the *grihastha dharma*.

Then Brahma said to the Vanikas, 'I am telling you your *dharma*. You should bathe in the morning and the afternoon, propitiate your ancestors, recite the *namaskara mantra*, perform the five *yajnas*[1] and serve the Brahmans. You should constantly look after their affairs and serve them. O Shudras! You should always serve the Brahmans without any arrogance.' Having given these commands, the three gods gave land and houses to the Vanikas.

Thus till the end of Kritayuga, the Brahmans and Vanikas stayed in Dharmaranya. According to *dharma* (moral order) the Brahmans were engaged in the reading of the Vedas, contemplation of philosophy, performance of sacrifices and devotion to the gods. Those Brahmans who were not clever enough to devote themselves to

---

[1] The householder is enjoined to perform five *yajnas* every day. These are (1) fire-sacrifice to beings, (2) fire-sacrifice to men, (3) fire-sacrifice to ancestors, (4) fire-sacrifice to gods, and (5) fire-sacrifice to the Brahman.

learning and who had no inclination for the Vedas and holy sacrifices, became the domestic priests of the Vanikas. The Vanikas dutifully served the gods and thus both *varnas* lived happily. There was no mixture of *varnas* and Dharmaranya remained the purest place of pilgrimage on earth.

MYTH (3): *The Austerities of Dharmaraja*

This story starts with Yudhishthira asking, 'Why is the name of the place Dharmaranya? Where is the Dharmakupa [well of merit] in it?' Then Dhaumya narrates a story according to which the pilgrim centre got its name from Dharmaraja, the son of the Sun,[1] who performed severe penances there. The story goes as follows:

Once Dharmaraja, the ruler of the land of the dead, performed a severe austerity to please Shiva and see him in person. Indra, the ruler of heaven, was afraid that Dharmaraja was performing the austerity in order to gain the kingdom of heaven for himself. To divert Dharmaraja from his austerity, Indra sent his court-dancer, the beautiful Urvashi, to lure him away. When Urvashi came close to Dharmaraja, the cruel summer was replaced by spring, the season conducive to love. Thus Indra's strategy was complete.

Urvashi sang and danced around Dharmaraja to lure him, and after a long time Dharmaraja opened his eyes. He saw that spring had replaced summer which he knew was contrary to nature for that time of the year. Then he saw Urvashi and at once understood the aim of her visit. So he said to her, 'Why do you unnecessarily tire yourself, my child? I shall not be diverted from my penance. However, I am pleased with your singing and shall grant you a boon.' Urvashi begged him to abstain from asking for Indra's throne to which he replied that it had never been his intention to do so. He told her that he was performing the penance in order to see Shiva in person. Then Urvashi asked him to have a beautiful lake constructed there, which should be capable of destroying all sins and after bathing in which men should become free of all sorrows. Then she returned to heaven and related the whole story to Indra.

After Urvashi had left, Dharmaraja continued with his penance. It was a long time before he succeeded in pleasing Shiva who appeared in person before him. Dharmaraja worshipped and honoured him. Shiva offered him a boon and Dharmaraja requested that a

---

[1] Dharmaraja is the name of both Yama and Yudhishthira. In the myth, the reference is to Yama who was born of the Sun, and was the ruler of hell.

forest be named after him. He begged that a Shivalinga be established
there which should also bear his name. He made a further request
that Shiva and Parvati should always reside there; and those who
gave charities (*dana*) recited the name of god (*japa*), performed fire-
sacrifices (*homa*) and prayed at this place of pilgrimage, should always
profit in everything. Shiva granted him the boon and said that the
place where Dharmaraja had performed the penance would be known
as Dharmaranya after his name and that it would be the most
glorious pilgrim centre in the world.

MYTH (4): *The Story of Jayadeva*

Once a Brahman called Jayadeva killed another Brahman and appropriated his money. He cremated the body in a secluded place so that
no one would learn of his action. However, because of this sin he
was afflicted with leprosy. He went on many pilgrimages in order
to get cured, but he could not recover. After a long time he heard
of Dharmaranya. He went there and bathed in the lake and was
cured.

MYTH (5): *The Sorrows of Shrimata*

Once upon a time Rama visited Dharmaranya where he performed
the rituals of bathing in the sacred Dharmakupa, made oblations to
ancestors, and worshipped the Shivalinga. But he noticed that there
were no people there and asked his preceptor Vashishtha whether he
knew the whereabouts of the Brahmans and Gobhujas. Vashishtha
replied, 'O Rama! I do not know why the city is empty. Earlier when
I visited Moheraka, I saw Brahmans who are learned in the Vedas
and their servants here.'

At some time on the same night, Rama heard a woman's cries
from the southern direction. His curiosity was aroused and he sent
some servants to find out who the woman was and why she was
crying. When the servants went to her and asked her why she was
crying, she replied that she would tell her sorrows only to Rama. The
servants took her to Rama who bowed to her and asked her the
reason for her sorrow. After eulogizing the virtues of Rama, she
replied, 'O Rama! I was made the presiding deity of this city by
Brahma and I am known as Shrimata. But now that the city is
empty I do not know what to do.'

Rama said, 'Why is the city empty? Where have the Brahmans
gone? I do not know, so please tell me.'

Shrimata said, 'The Brahmans were tormented by the demons. They have therefore left the city and gone elsewhere.'

Rama said, 'O Shrimata, I do not know where these Brahmans have gone. I do not know their *gotras*, their number, their behaviour, or surnames—none of these do I know. Tell me all about this and then I shall send my servants to fetch them all.'

Shrimata said, 'Brahma, Vishnu and Mahesh established eighteen thousand Brahmans who were learned in the three Vedas. They have twenty-four *gotras* and forty-two surnames.' Then she recited these and said that the Modh Brahmans would be recognized by them. She further told Rama that the servants of the Brahmans, who were religious and devoted to the Brahmans, were also known as Modhs. She implored Rama to bring them back to Moheraka.

Rama sent his servants and messengers to bring the Brahmans there. The servants found the Brahmans and gave them Rama's message. They immediately came to Dharmaranya to see Rama. Rama begged them to tell him what services he could do for them. He also told them that he wanted to perform *yajnas* (holy-fire sacrifices) and requested them to accept his gifts.

The Brahmans consulted each other and then some of them said, 'O Rama! We make our livelihood by *shilocha*, i.e. we do not accept gifts.' Others said, 'O King! We are *kumbhidhanya*—we only accumulate food to last us for six days.' Still others said that they accumulated food only to last them for one day. Others said that they ate only dry leaves and fruit that had fallen from trees. They all said that they had been established there by Brahma, Vishnu, and Mahesh, and could accept nothing without their command.

On hearing this from the Brahmans, Rama closed his eyes and thought of the three gods. At once, Brahma, Vishnu, and Mahesh appeared and Rama said to them, 'O Gods! These Brahmans do not accept any gifts. Please command them to accept my gifts so that my task is accomplished. I have been ordered by Shrimata to rescue these poor people.'

The gods eulogized Rama in various ways. They told the Brahmans that they should have no hesitation in accepting gifts from Rama, since Rama was a god himself. Then all the preparations for the fire-sacrifices were made and after the performance of the fire-sacrifices Rama gave fifty villages to the Trivedi Modh Brahmans. Then Hanumana was sent to call the Gobhuja Vanikas, established there, to serve the Brahmans and they were given land and houses of their own. Having ordered the Gobhujas to serve the Brahmans, Rama gave them a bright sword and a white *chamar* (a yak-tail switch) and said that every bridegroom must carry these on the auspicious occasion of his marriage. He further said that on every auspicious occasion the Brahmans must be worshipped and *dakshina* (fee for the officiating priests) must be given. He exhorted the Vanikas to obey the Brahmans and to worship them on auspicious as well as inauspicious occasions. Rama also gave the one and a quarter lakh Shudras, who had come with him from Mandal village, to the Brahmans so that the Shudras might serve them. These Mandalikas were also known as Modhs by Rama's command.

Having done all this, Rama began to perform *vastu puja* (a ritual performed before inauguration). However, all the signs were inauspicious. The fire would not take the oblation, the Brahmans could not recite the *mantras* (sacred verses) and the gods were not favourably inclined. Rama asked Vashishtha the reason for these inauspicious signs. Vashishtha thought this over and then divined the cause, that the Vaishnavi Goddess Paramaranda had not been worshipped. Then Rama worshipped Paramaranda with reverence and when she was pleased the *vastu puja* was performed properly.

Yudhishthira said to Dhaumya, 'It is surprising that when Rama was himself the sacrificer, there were obstacles to the sacrifice. Please tell me who Paramaranda is, where she was born and why she was granted a boon by Brahma.' Then Dhaumya related the story of Paramaranda, as follows:

Once Vishnu was sleeping at Prayaga. From his yawn was born the attractive Shakti (female divinity) who reverentially worshipped the Lord of the World. When Vishnu did not speak to her even after a long time had elapsed, Brahma who was sitting nearby said to her, 'O *Devi*! I am pleased with your devotion to Vishnu. So ask for a boon.' Paramaranda said, 'O Lord! If you are pleased with me, then instruct me on the kind of life I should lead, the work I should do, and please give me a name'. Brahma then gave her the name Paramaranda and said that Trivedis would always worship her on auspicious occasions. He related the mode of her worship and said that if the Trivedi Modhs did not worship her, there would be many obstacles in their path.

The goddess Paramaranda having been propitiated, Rama performed the fire-sacrifice and fed the Brahmans. He established the goddess Shrimata there along with the other gods. He had deep wells constructed and the city was made even more beautiful than before. He fed the Brahmans and gave them many gifts. He gave them gifts of cows, land, gold, clothes, chariots, horses, and elephants. Then Rama gave away fifty villages to the Trivedi Brahmans. Though he offered gifts of villages to the Chaturvedi Brahmans, they refused to accept them. They said, 'We have been established by Brahma, Vishnu, and Mahesh. O Rama! We will not accept any charity from you.' Rama heard them and ruminated over what they had said but, because he was afraid of having a curse put on him, he did not say anything in reply.

Rama wrote his command clearly on a copperplate and gave it to the Trivedis. For their protection he entrusted them to Hanumana. Rama told Hanumana that he would have to stay in Moheraka and preside over marriages and disputes. He was to protect Brahmans from demons and if anyone were to defy Rama's command, then Hanumana was to punish him. Then Rama, being pleased, gave the sword and the yak-tail switch to the Mandalikas so that they could wear these on the occasion of their marriage ceremonies.

After this, Rama again went on various pilgrimages and then came back to Moheraka with his army. Seeing the Brahmans who were learned in the Vedas, Rama thought of performing a fire-sacrifice. When all the preparations were made, Sita said to Rama, 'O Rama! Please call those Brahmans whom you had established earlier.' The Brahmans came and conducted the fire-sacrifice, and were given *dakshina*.

After this the Chaturvedi Brahmans said to Rama, 'O Rama! We did not accept your charity earlier. Therefore, the Trivedi Brahmans intimidate us all the time. We will leave Moheraka and go elsewhere.' Then Sita said to Rama, 'Please settle a village here and give it my name. I shall give that village to the Modh Brahmans and then the Chaturvedis shall stay here.'

Rama called some good architects and asked them to construct a beautiful village there. This village was known as Sitapur. Rama gave the Chaturvedi Brahmans this village along with other gifts and, obeying Sita's command, the Brahmans accepted the gifts.

Yudhishthira asked Dhaumya, 'After having devotedly worshipped the eighteen thousand Brahmans, how did Rama divide the villages which he gave in charity? By nature Brahmans always oppose each other. How did they stay there without opposing each other?'

Dhaumya replied that the Brahmans' faults of anger and jealousy were wiped away by Rama's words. Therefore the Brahmans accepted whichever villages were given to them during the sacrifice. Each Brahman took his own share and the rules of good conduct were not broken. Rama gave these villages to Modh Brahmans for their residence and the Chaturvedi Modhs stayed in their own villages. They were given the names of the villages from which they came and were known by their *gotras* and *pravaras*.[1] It was only through fate that after a while the Brahmans' conduct became disreputable. They polluted the villages, were out of work, and started opposing each other.

Having established the Brahmans, Rama returned with Sita to his capital and left Hanumana to look after the Modh Brahmans. For some time the Brahmans, Gobhujas, and Mandalikas stayed together in peace without any malice. The Vanikas served the Brahmans and each *varna* thought of the welfare of the others.

MYTH (6): *The Story of King Aama*

At the end of Dvapara age, there was a king called Aama who ruled the kingdom of Kanyakubja.[2] This brave king gave up the Vedic religion and became a Bauddha. Since the king became a believer in the religion of Kaliyuga, his conduct became sinful. The king's subjects followed him and they were also converted to the religion of Kaliyuga.

The king had a beautiful daughter, born under the auspicious stars, who was known by the name of Ratnaganga. When she grew up the king gave her in marriage to a prince called Brahmavrata. After the marriage, her father presented her with Dharmaranya and Moheraka, where she set up her residence.

One day the princess called all the Brahmans and asked them to vacate the villages which had been given to them by earlier kings. She said, 'The land belongs to us now and we shall not let the Brahmans enjoy its fruits. Our *tirthankaras* [Jain mendicants] who eat little, and who have no attachments are to be worshipped. The Brahmans are greedy and they indulge in violence. Therefore they are not revered. You may live in this country or go elsewhere—but

---

[1] *Gotras* refer to loose exogamous groups among the Brahmans which trace fictitious descent from ancient sages. *Pravara* is any noble ancestor who contributes to the credit of a *gotra*.

[2] For reasons which will become clear later, we have kept as close as possible to the Sanskrit original in translating this story. This has necessarily made the English rendering rather awkward.

you will not get our patronage.' Saying this, she, the embodiment of sin, who had been inspired by her wicked ministers, took away the land which had been given by Rama to the Brahmans. The Brahmans showed her the copperplate given by Rama making the grant. But she said, 'You go to the kingdom of Ramachandra. This land belongs to me now and the *Tirthankaras* are the ones who deserve worship from me, not these deceitful Brahmans.' Having said this to the Brahmans, she bade her servants destroy the *yupa* (sacrificial pillars) and to construct Jain temples there.

The unhappy Brahmans consulted each other and decided that it would not be wise to live in a place where the Vedic religion was being destroyed and a heretical religion established. They therefore decided to go to Kanyakubja to show the king the copperplate which had been given to them by Rama. Travelling through various cities, they finally reached the capital of King Aama which was full of sinful Jain-renouncers who were denouncing the Vedic religion. They went to the king's court and were shown in by the gatekeeper. They saw the king, and giving him their blessings, they said, 'O Fortunate One! May all that is good be yours. May you live long and happily. May you do good to your people and may you protect your kingdom and make it stable.'

The king saw those tired Brahmans who had travelled far to reach his kingdom and addressed them thus, 'Who are you? Where do you stay? What do you want from us? For what have you come here, you killers of animals?[1] You, who cheat stupid people, eat everything greedily, always accept gifts from others, are wicked and slaves of your senses; why have you come here?'

The Brahmans replied, 'O King! Our houses were in the meritorious Moheraka which is in Dharmaranya. Shri Ramachandra established us there. Earlier we were created by Brahma, Vishnu, and Mahesh, and settled in that beautiful town which was created by their command. As time passed, the town Moheraka was destroyed. Rama relieved the sufferers and gave villages and wealth to the chief Brahmans. He engraved his command on a copperplate and gave it to us. Accordingly, earlier kings protected us during their regimes. Now your daughter has come to our city and has appropriated the grants given to us by Ramachandra. We have heard that you are a righteous king (*dharmaraja*), and have come to you. Please protect

[1] This is a reference to the sacrifice of animals which was necessary for certain Vedic rituals.

us and enjoy your kingdom for a long time to come. This life is as fickle as water that has fallen on a leaf. You who know the essence—follow the *dharma* by which one increases one's life. Mandhata and Harishchandra died after having ruled the earth. None of these kings could take away their kingdoms with them. Whatever charity has been given to a *bhikshuka* [literally, beggar], that is not taken away even by Mlechas [non-Aryans], what to speak of Shudras and Kshatriyas. You are a righteous king. Do you want to become rich by taking away a *bhikshuka's* property? O best of kings, protect the Brahmans according to the commands of Ramachandra. Become like *dharma* incarnate and acquire merit from today. Whether the king is a Kshatriya or a Shudra, it is his duty to protect the Brahmans.'

Then the king asked, 'Who was this Ramachandra who gave you this grant?' The Brahmans replied, 'Rama was born in the Surya Vansha [sun-lineage] and he was Dasharatha's son. He took birth as a human being in order to kill Ravana. He gave those villages as a grant to us.'

The king said, 'There were many kings who were very brave. Whosoever the king is, the land belongs to him. When Rama was the king of the whole earth, he gave the villages to the Brahmans. Now the earth belongs to me. Why should I recognize his grant now? Just as I am a king now, he was a king then. Without a part of Vishnu in him, no one can become the Lord of Earth.

'Happiness and sorrow are emotions felt by all human beings. What was so great about Rama? Due to his sorrow he went to the forest and he killed the man who kidnapped his wife. He had to undergo many difficulties because of Ravana. Rama was just a man and I do not see anything extraordinary about him. So why should I protect the grant given by him? If there is any divine sign which can persuade me immediately to believe in Rama, then show me that sign. If Rama appointed Hanumana to protect you, then bring him to me.

'All the *shastras* say that non-violence is the ultimate righteousness. Then why do you call the Jain religion a heretic religion? All our preceptors are without a trace of violence and are full of compassion. The Brahmans are always desiring sensuous pleasures and all of them are bent on committing violence. They are full of desires, prone to anger, and are greedy. Tell me which of their virtues should make me worship them? Men have to bear the results of their good and bad actions. Happiness and unhappiness are both attained by our actions. Rama also was born because of his *karmas* [past actions] and died because of them. He had happiness and sorrow. What is extraordinary about him that he should be remembered?

'You have a family, you fall ill and so do we. So what is the difference between the worshipper and the worshipped? Some people live by their brains and others by their strength. These are two ways to make a living in the world. Which one of these is preferable to you? What virtue do you have that you are ready to enjoy these villages? The Brahmans should not accumulate property. So the ownership of villages will send you to hell.

'Kings should protect their people, Vaishyas should trade, and Shudras should serve others. This has been decided by the Dharmashastras.

'Those who know the Vedas say that in earlier times the whole earth was given by Parshurama to a Brahman called Kashyapa. Then how did Rama rule the earth? When the earth actually belonged to someone else, then how was it given to you by Rama? And how did you, who are keen to be righteous, accept the gift? Therefore you have indulged in sinful actions and Rama was not the protector of *dharma*.'

The Brahmans replied, 'It is said in the Vedas that non-violence is the supreme duty. But violence is not always to be abhorred, and when performed in a sacrifice it leads to heaven. No one can be completely non-violent. Violence is everywhere and therefore, whatever the Jain renouncers say is blind arrogance. Can anyone keep alive without eating and how is food to be got without violence? Is there anyone on earth who does not have a tendency towards violence? O King! people live by violence alone. If fruit growing on trees is eaten, violence is done to the birds by taking away their means of living. When water, food, and leaves are left overnight, then insects are bred in them and they die.

'All your Jain renouncers are full of anger and jealousy. They eat tasty foods and are still called *yatis* [ascetics]. They talk of love and romance to women. They are full of greed, avarice, animosity, and arrogance. Who would call them *yatis*?

'Violence can be of various types, O King! It is difficult to ascertain the subtle differences between them, especially in the Kaliyuga. When a man thinks ill of others, he commits mental violence. Yet can man completely control his thoughts? If a person thinks of his good qualities and thinks badly of others—then also he commits violence.

When someone hurts others by being rude, then he is committing violence through words. When someone places obstacles in others' paths to get his own work done, is that not violence?

'O King! *yatis* are those who are above happiness and sorrow and are not influenced by praise or insults. We [i.e. those who have been successful in controlling their senses] are the followers of the *grihastha-dharma*[1] [dharma of householder] and are experts in the learning of Vedas and Vedangas. We are engrossed in our own work and are without anger or malice. Therefore, O King, protect the Brahmans according to Rama's command and it will bring prosperity to you.'

The king, however, insisted that the Brahmans should give him some proof of Rama's divinity or they should present Hanumana in person to him. He promised that if they could fulfil any of these conditions then he would return the villages to them and would himself be reconverted to the Vedic religion. The Brahmans, having promised that they would produce Hanumana in his court, returned to Moheraka.

After returning to Moheraka, an argument ensued between the Trivedi and the Chaturvedi Brahmans on the advisability of trying to see Hanumana in person by pleasing him through meditation and penance. The Trivedis felt that since the Brahmans had lost their power to curse in the Kaliyuga, they could only secure their grants by pleasing Hanumana. He would appear in person to them and convince the king of the divinity of Rama. The Chaturvedis, on the other hand, advocated the theory of fate and argued that the Brahmans should be content with whatever fate had decreed for them and instead of trying to convince the king to return their villages, they should adopt the *vritti* (source of livelihood) of the Vanikas. After much argument, the Trivedis and most of the Chaturvedis decided to send their representatives to the forest, where they would meditate and try to propitiate Hanumana. Because of the hardships they had had to endure in the forest, the representatives of the Chaturvedis decided to abandon the pursuit and so they returned without having accomplished their mission.

The Trivedis continued on the hazardous journey and finally, through severe austerities and genuine devotion, succeeded in pleasing Hanumana. Thus propitiated, he appeared in person to

[1] This is the first time in the text that Brahmans are mentioned as followers of the *grihastha dharma*.

them. When they told him their story, he gave them two small parcels of his hair and said that the parcel containing the hair from his left side was to be shown to the king as a sign that they had themselves seen Hanumana. When the king disbelieved them, they were to throw it on the ground and put a curse on him that his palace and his entire army would burn. Then they were to come out of the palace. Following the curse, a terrible fire would rage in the palace, and the king's entire army would be burnt. The king would rush to the Brahmans and falling at their feet he would ask for their forgiveness. Then they were to give him the second parcel containing the hair from his right side which would revive his fallen soldiers.

Having told the Brahmans this, Hanumana disappeared. The tired Brahmans were carried back to Moheraka by Maruta, the Wind God, who was the father of Hanumana. There the representatives of the Trivedi Brahmans related the entire story to the other Brahmans and then they happily started for the capital of King Aama.

Events followed in the exact order predicted by Hanumana and when the king's army was revived he was very pleased with the Brahmans. He turned out all the heretical Jains from the city. He threw all their books into the river and declared that those who would give shelter to the heretical Jains would be punished and turned out of the city.

Then the king told the Brahmans that he would like to perform the appropriate acts of penance for his earlier conduct. They suggested that he should do so by the performance of fire-sacrifices. They also asked him to give in charity, perform austerities, worship Brahmans and be steadfast in his devotion to Vishnu. The king performed all these acts. Then he wished to give more gifts to the Brahmans but they said that as long as the villages given by Rama were not taken away by the King they did not want anything else. The king bade farewell to them and they returned joyously to Moheraka.

II

In this section the individual myths shall be analysed and in the next an integrated discussion of the results obtained here will be undertaken. The first myth starts with the creation of the world, but there is a sudden break in the story and the author switches over from the creation of the physical world to the creation of Brahmans in

Dharmaranya. Apparently the part relating to the creation of the physical world cannot be satisfactorily analysed here since it is not given in sufficient detail and serves only as a prologue to the latter part of the story.

Therefore, if we leave this part of the first myth and compare the first two stories, we find that there are three kinds of statements being made about the categories of Brahmans and Vanikas. These are: (i) the reasons for the creation of Brahmans and Vanikas, (ii) the process of their creation, and (iii) the characteristics of Brahmans and Vanikas. An analysis of these statements gives us the meaning of the categories Brahman and Vanika/Shudra.

The first myth deals with the reasons for the creation of Brahmans. It is to be noted that this story is not explicitly about the creation of Brahmans but about the creation of Dharmaranya. The title of the story makes this quite clear and in fact the story is concluded by Dhaumya saying, 'Thus the way the greatest of the *tirthas* [pilgrim centres] was created has been recited by me.' The Brahmans are created by the three gods so that the place Dharmaranya can become a *tirtha*, 'fit for the gods to reside in'. Thus the creation of the Brahmans transforms a mere physical space into a *tirtha*, which is a category of social space. The creation by Brahma is limited to the creation of the physical world through increasing differentiation and it is only after the creation of the Brahmans that *social* space as distinct from *physical* space is created. Therefore, the Brahmans mediate between the physical and the social. Thus in its most general meaning, the term Brahman is equivalent to transformer of the *physical* and the *social*.

If we now turn to the characteristics of the Brahmans and Vanikas respectively as described in the myth, it is easy to show that these are in a relation of opposition to each other. The activities of the Brahmans are described as pursuit of knowledge, performance of holy sacrifices, devotion to God, teaching, and advising on matters relating to political ethics. These activities, which may be briefly summed up as contemplative activities, are described as the *dharma* (duty) of the Brahmans. Further, the Brahmans are owners of property bequeathed to them by the gods but are neither the managers nor are they expected to use this property for purposes of accumulation. Any reference to women belonging to the Brahman *varna* and marriage of Brahmans is absent. This absence is conspicuous when compared to the origin of Vanikas for whom women of the same category are immediately created and to whom they are married. In the case of the Brahmans it is clear that mechanisms of succession and inheritance are not maintained through sexual reproduction.

The Vanikas (the word is used interchangeably with the word Shudra) are created specifically for the purposes of managing the property of the Brahmans, so that the latter can be left free to pursue their contemplative activities. Their *dharma*, as described by the gods, consists of a few simple rituals, like reciting the *namaskara mantra*, performing the five *yajnas*, and propitiating ancestors. These rituals are recognized in other Sanskrit texts as the *dharma* of the householder.[1] As soon as the Vanikas are created they ask God about the means through which their *vansha* (lineage) would increase. Then women of the same *varna* are created for them, to whom they are married, so that they may be able to pursue the *grihastha dharma*. In this case, then, procreation is mentioned as a duty of the Vanikas and succession-inheritance is through sexual reproduction.

The characteristics of the Brahmans and Vanika/Shudras can be schematically represented as follows:

Brahmans	Vanika/Shudras
(1) *dharma* to engage in contemplative activities	*dharma* consisting of householders' rituals
(2) owners of property but not managers	managers as well as owners of property
(3) no marriage	endogamous marriage
(4) succession-inheritance not by birth	succession-inheritance by birth

We now propose to show that the characteristics of the Brahmans are in opposition to the characteristics of the Vanika/Shudra category and that, taken together, these represent an opposition between non-householders and householders.

That the *dharma* of the Brahmans and the *dharma* of the Vanikas are in opposition to each other is one of the premises of the myths. The second myth (Creation of the Vanikas) relates how the Brahmans were engaged in contemplative activities and, therefore, had no time to manage either their property or their household affairs. In fact the Brahmans explicitly reject the possibility of their becoming

---

[1] Performance of the five *yajnas* is one of the duties of the householder which is stressed in the Grihya Sutras. Similarly the Grihya Sutra enjoins the periodic propitiation of ancestors on the householder.

involved in these affairs, 'for household affairs awaken desire and greed, and once greed is awakened, where is *dharma* and where is knowledge?', and in this they have the approval of the gods. Thus involvement in household affairs is seen in opposition to contemplative activities and, therefore, the two are treated as mutually exclusive. Hence the *dharma* of those who are involved in contemplative activities is in opposition to the *dharma* of those who are involved in household affairs.

In this context the second characteristic of Brahmans and Vanikas respectively is extremely interesting for it represents an opposition in the relationship of each category to property. Brahmans own property but are not expected either to manage it or to use it for the accumulation of wealth. Their relationship to property, therefore, is that of non-involvement and non-accumulation. Vanikas, on the other hand, are created for the purpose of managing the property of Brahmans and hence have an active involvement with property. They are themselves given land and houses by the gods and, as we shall show later, are created from the symbol of prosperity. Hence their relationship to property is that of involvement and accumulation, which is in opposition to the relationship of Brahmans to property.

The third and the fourth characteristics of Brahmans and Vanikas are more obviously in opposition to each other. Absence of marriage characterizes non-householders while endogamous marriage is essential for householders in the *ashrama* ideology. Similarly, non-householders perpetuate themselves through means other than physical propagation—like voluntary recruitment or in some myths by non-sexual reproduction. The householders, on the other hand, perpetuate themselves through physical propagation and procreation of sons is an important duty of the householder.

It is obvious that the series of oppositions enumerated above, when taken together, express a fundamental opposition between non-householders and householders. From this we get the relation:

(Brahman: Vanik) $\simeq$ (non-householder: householder)

Now to make the two sides of this relation comparable we shall have to substitute native categories for non-householder and householder. The term for householder is given by the myth itself, when it describes the Vanikas as followers of *grihastha dharma* which is the second stage in a Hindu's life according to *ashrama* ideology. We will now have to substitute a category for non-householder which is in opposition to *grihastha* in terms of the logic of *ashrama* ideology.

Ashrama ideology is often characterized as dividing the individual life-span into four successive stages: *brahmacharya* (of the student), *garhasthya* (of the householder), *vanaprastha* (of the hermit) and *sanyasa* (of the ascetic). (See de Bary, 1958: 230–5.) The first stage is preparatory to the second; in the second the individual marries, begets children, and follows an occupation. The third stage is one of transition between the second, in which an individual is a householder, and the fourth, in which the individual prepares himself for total renunciation. At this stage of life a man is expected to retire from active family and social life but he should be available for providing advice and guidance to members of his family whenever they need him. He is expected either to take his wife with him or commit her to the care of his sons. In the last stage the individual renounces the world totally and has no rights and obligations either as a member of his *varna* or his household. His renunciation as a member of his *varna* is symbolized by his giving up the sacred thread and the break with his family is symbolized by the performance of his funeral rites by his immediate kin. After this he is considered to be symbolically dead to his family and caste.

Though the four *ashramas* are usually represented as four successive stages, it may be more profitable to think of them as *statuses*, for it is not obligatory for an individual to leave the first stage (as the word *balabrahmachari*, i.e. *brahmachari* since childhood, denotes) or reach the fourth stage only after having passed the first three stages. Conceived of as *statuses*, it seems probable that the *ashramas* result from a division of the universe into cross-cutting categories of *varna*/ non-*varna* and householder/non-householder. In terms of these fundamental oppositions, we can characterize the *ashramas* as follows:

	Varnatva	*Garhasthya*
brahmachari	+	—
grihastha	+	+
vanaprastha	—	+
sanyasi	—	—

A *brahmachari* belongs to a *varna* but is not a householder. A *grihastha* belongs to a *varna* and is a householder. A *vanaprasthi* gives up his *varna* obligations by physically moving out of the social order to a hermitage and also giving up many of his obligations as a house-holder, but since he is permitted to retire with his wife, his status as a householder cannot be denoted by a negative. A *sanyasi* renounces the world completely and has no rights and obligations either as a member of his *varna* or as a householder.

It should be clear from the schematic representation that the main opposition in the *ashrama* ideology is between *garhasthya* and *sanyasa*, the former being a category which represents the social and the latter representing the asocial. *Vanaprastha* logically and actually mediates between *garhasthya* and *sanyasa*, which is why it juxtaposes within itself opposite characteristics, some belonging to the *grihastha ashrama* and others to *sanyasa*. *Brahmacharya* is the inverse of *vanaprastha*, since it also has one positive and one negative sign but the signs are inverted. We hope it is sufficiently clear that in terms of the logic of *ashrama* ideology, the opposite term of *grihastha* is *sanyasi*, and substituting these for householder and non-householder respectively, we get the following relation:

> (Brahman: Vanika) $\simeq$ (*sanyasi: grihastha*).

This means that the category Brahman is in opposition to the cate-gory Vanika here and *in relation to the Vanika, the Brahman is parallel[1] to the sanyasi.*

We now come to the way in which each category originated. The Brahmans are created from the mouth of the gods, a theme familiar in other myths,[2] and as indicated earlier, they transform the physical into the social.

The Vanikas are created through the agency of the divine cow who kicks the earth from which they arise. Here we have two statements which have to be explained: first, their rising from the earth, and second, the meaning of earth being kicked by a cow. In this context, we would also have to explain the mode of creation of the Vanika women who are created by Vishvavasu Gandharva.

In the Sanskritic tradition, the dust which rises when the cow kicks the earth is a symbol of prosperity[3] and clearly the Vanikas are created from the symbol of prosperity. As regards the Vanika women, they are created by Vishvavasu Gandharva, who is the pre-

---

[1] Parallelism is being used to denote similarity but not identity.

[2] This theme first occurs in the Purusha Sukta hymn in the Rigveda.

[3] The Vishnu Purana, for instance, says that prosperity dwells in the dust arising from a cow's couch.

siding deity of procreation.[1] These symbols define the main activities of the Vanikas—their duties to procreate and accumulate wealth through management of property—which are the duties of a householder. The conclusion arrived at here corroborates the conclusions arrived at earlier about the characteristics of the Vanikas.

The second point of inquiry is the meaning of the reference to Vanikas' rising from the earth. There seems very little doubt that by this statement the author is opposing the Vanikas with a second, implicit category, that of the *sanyasi.* Though in continental India, cremation is the standard mode for the disposal of the dead among Hindus, the *sanyasi* is never cremated but is buried in a sitting position (Kane, 1941, vol. II, pt. II: 965). Therefore, the coming up of the Vanikas from the earth is in opposition to the *sanyasi*'s going down into the earth.

At this point it would be worth stating the main points that have emerged from the analysis of the first two myths. The myths have been interpreted to define the meaning of the categories Brahman, and Vanika/Shudra. As a latent term, the *sanyasi* is brought in and provides points for parallelism or opposition with the stated terms. The term Brahman, in its most general meaning, is equivalent to transformer of physical into social. Its more specific meaning is in relation to the category Vanika/Shudra, and is expressed from the following relation which we obtained from the myth and the logic of *ashrama* ideology:

$$(\text{Brahman: Vanika}) \simeq (\text{non-householder: householder})$$
$$\simeq (sanyasi: grihastha).$$

Finally, it was found that in understanding the meaning of the symbolic statement that Vanikas rose from the earth, we had to oppose the Vanikas to the latent term, *sanyasi.* Since the word Vanika has been used interchangeably with the word Shudra in these two myths, and since the myths clearly define the category as belonging to the *varna* order and the *grihastha ashrama,* it would be fair to conclude that the term Vanika/Shudra refers to categories other than Brahmans within the social order of *varna* and householdership. Therefore, the opposition of *sanyasi* to this category, in fact, expresses an opposition between *sanyasi* and categories other than Brahmans within the social order of *varna* and householdership.

[1] The Gandharva Vishvavasu is mentioned as the presiding deity of procreation in Winternitz (1966, vol. II: 229).

We now come to the third myth, 'The Penance of Dharmaraja'. This myth is clearly concerned with defining the meaning of *sanyasa*. A condensed summary of the myth including the principal characters and events is given in Chart 1 on the facing page. The events in the chart when read along each row refer to the chronological order in which they appear in the story, while each column refers to events or characters pertaining to the same structural theme. The conclusions emerging from each column are listed at the bottom.

The characters of the first column bring into focus the social distinctions of power/powerlessness and male/female. Indra and Dharmaraja have different domains of power, but the fact that there is a concept of power implies the opposite concept of powerlessness. We have called this distinction *social*, since the ruler, who represents legitimate power (as distinct from mere force), is a social category. Secondly, there is a clear distinction between male/female, but this distinction also is not merely physical for, by characterizing Urvashi as a seductress, a social meaning is being given to the female who seduces and the male who is seduced.

The second column brings out the different kinds of power that the ruler and the *sanyasi* have. Indra is apprehensive about Dharmaraja's practice of austerities because the esoteric power derived from them can be translated into political power. His attempt to lure Dharmaraja away from his penance through Urvashi is, in fact, an attempt to forestall the possibility of Dharmaraja usurping his throne. Thus, while the king has political power, the *sanyasi* can acquire esoteric power which can be transformed into political power.

The third column defines the characteristics of a *sanyasi*. The first statement, in this column, shows that *sanyasa* is a voluntaristic category. That Dharamaraja, the king of a certain domain, can practice austerities signifies that the role of the *sanyasi* is not pre-determined but can be assumed at will. However, during the period of *sanyasa*, the *sanyasi* has to be above the power/no power and male/female distinctions. The second statement clearly shows that Dharmaraja is not interested in power, but it would be a mistake to characterize him as powerless for, as the second column shows, he has potential power. Further, Dharmaraja does not get seduced by Urvashi. This shows that while he is not above the physical distinction of male/female since he is not an asexual character, he is above this distinction in social terms. Thus the third column first shows that *sanyasa* is a voluntaristic category, and then establishes the *asocial*

CHART 1

(1)	(2)	(3)	(4)	(5)
. Dharmaraja is the ruler of hell.		Dharmaraja, the ruler of hell, practises austerities.		
" Indra is the ruler of heaven.	Indra is apprehensive of Dharmaraja practising austerities, lest he usurp Indra's throne.	Dharmaraja has no intention of usurping Indra's throne.		Urvashi asks Dharmaraja to have a lake constructed there which should expiate the sins of men who bathe in it.
. Urvashi is a seductress.	Indra sends Urvashi to lure Dharmaraja away from his austerities.	Dharmaraja is not lured by Urvashi.	Dharmaraja grants a boon to Urvashi.	Dharmaranya is named after Dharmaraja and Shiva invests it with purificatory powers.
			Shiva is pleased with Dharmaraja. He appears in person to him and grants him a boon.	
Social distinctions of power/powerlessness, male/female.	Esoteric power can be transformed into political power.	Sanyasa s a voluntaristic category. Sanyasi is above social distinctions of power / powerlessness, and male/female.	Sanyasa forces gods to come in a relation with the sanyasi.	Dharmaranya has the two properties of a pilgrimage centre: (1) expiatory, and (2) purificatory.

character of the *sanyasi* by placing him above the power/powerless-ness, and male/female distinctions.

The fourth column brings out the relation between *sanyasi* and gods, which, as we shall show later, is different from that between Brahman and gods. Urvashi's failure to lure Dharmaraja away is the first step towards his success in *sanyasa* and she is, in fact, being rewarded for her failure. Had she succeeded in luring Dharmaraja away, he would have ceased to be a *sanyasi*. If successful, the *sanyasi forces* the gods to come into a relationship with him and this theme of the *sanyasi* pleasing the gods and getting whatever boon he desires is a very familiar one to students of Hindu mythology.

The last column explains the characteristics of Dharmaranya, which, as we have already noted, is a *tirtha*. It has a lake which is given expiatory powers by the *sanyasi*, and it also has purificatory powers, invested in it by Shiva. Clearly it becomes invested with these properties through the success of the *sanyasi* for, as we have already noted, the two events in column 4 mark stages in the success of Dharmaraja in his *sanyasa*, and it is at these points that Dharmaranya comes to have these properties. Incidentally, here we have a double opposition in which a pure place is first opposed to non-pure places and then the opposite properties of the pure place—expiatory powers (which are negative in that they remove sins) and purificatory powers (which are positive in that they confer merit)—are explained.

In the next myth, the story of Jayadeva, which is very brief, there is a direct confrontation between the powers of the Brahman and the powers of the *sanyasi*. In this story, Jayadeva suffers from leprosy because he has killed a Brahman. It is significant that he is not dis-covered and then punished, but suffers from this disease as a result of his sin. The myth clearly shows that every Brahman has certain inherent spiritual powers and that if his person is violated certain spontaneous reflex sanctions[1] are set in motion and the offender is automatically punished. Now, what cures Jayadeva is a bath in the lake in Dharmaranya which, as we know from the earlier myth, had been invested with expiatory powers by the *sanyasi*. Thus the Brah-man's inherent punitive powers are opposed to the *sanyasi*'s acquired expiatory powers and the latter is shown to be stronger. This myth therefore defines the different kinds of spiritual powers of Brahman and *sanyasi*—the former has spiritual merit, inherent in his position, which gives him punitive powers and the latter has acquired spiritual

[1] This term is being used in the sense proposed by Radcliffe-Brown (1933).

merit which gives him expiatory powers. This may be expressed by the relation

(Brahman: *sanyasi*) $\simeq$ (Inherent spiritual merit: Acquired spiritual merit) $\simeq$ (Punitive powers: Expiatory powers).

Since the relation between punitive powers and expiatory powers is a relation of opposition, we conclude that inherent spiritual merit is opposed to acquired spiritual merit and finally Brahman is opposed to *sanyasi*.

We shall now proceed to an analysis of the next myth, 'The Sorrows of Shrimata'. For purposes of analysis, it is essential to divide the myth into two parts—the first part relating to events preceding the sacrifice made by Rama in which the Brahmans officiated, and the second part relating to events which followed the sacrifice. In what follows we shall try to show that this myth introduces the principle of temporal power and establishes the relation between king who represents temporal power, and Brahman, who, as demonstrated earlier, represents inherent spiritual merit. Finally, we shall show that the relation between king and Brahman is discussed in the myth with reference to the third neutral term *sanyasi*, which remains latent in the myth. In the first part of the myth the events relating to Rama (who is addressed as king) and the Brahmans are as follows:

RAMA. Comes with his army to Moheraka/wishes to perform a sacrifice to propitiate gods and ancestors/needs the help of Brahmans who have to officiate in the sacrifice to make it acceptable to the gods and ancestors.

BRAHMANS. Have been forced to leave Moheraka because *rakshasas* (demons) trouble them/are asked to perform sacrifice since this would necessarily entail their acceptance of gifts as *dakshina* (fee for officiating priests) and *dana* (gifts of charity) from Rama.

It should be quite clear from the summary discussion above that Rama, as king, has temporal power but cannot acquire spiritual merit without the help of Brahmans. The Brahmans, on the other hand, have inherent spiritual merit as shown earlier but they have no temporal power which is why they cannot protect themselves from demons. The relation between the Brahmans and the king is that of independence.

In the second part, the events are as follows:

RAMA. Succeeds in getting the consent of some Brahmans to officiate in a sacrifice performed by him/worships Paramaranda, the goddess of the Brahmans/writes his grant on a copperplate and leaves Hanumana to protect the Brahmans.

BRAHMANS. Some Brahmans agree to perform the sacrifice for Rama/ are given gifts of land/the grant is documented and given to them as proof of their right to the use of the land.

In the second part of the story, the relation of the Brahmans to the king changes. They officiate for the king in a sacrifice and thus, *in relation to the king*, become mediators between the king and gods/ ancestors. In exchange the king gives them grants of land which obviously belongs to the king. The complete spiritual dependence of the king on the Brahmans is demonstrated by his having to worship the caste goddess of the Brahmans. The complete temporal dependence of the Brahmans on the king is demonstrated by their having to accept the grants from the king. Thus a relationship of exchange resulting in mutual dependence is established between them.

The relation of the Vanika/Shudra category to the Brahmans continues to be the same though they are also now established by the king. However, the exhortation of Rama to the Vanikas to worship the Brahmans on all auspicious and inauspicious occasions adds a new dimension to the relation between Brahmans and Vanikas/Shudras. If we interpret the auspicious and inauspicious occasions to mean the various rites of transition, like birth, marriage, death, etc. in the life of an individual, then it seems probable that the Brahmans also mediate on the rites of passage of the non-Brahman householders within the *varna* system.

There is one fact of importance which we shall take up later, viz. that some Brahmans refuse to officiate for the king in the beginning and the king admits his helplessness in persuading them to do so. It is only later that these Brahmans (the Chaturved's) agree to officiate for the king and accept grants from him. Finally, we shall show in the next section that the relation between the king and the Brahmans is established with reference to the third neutral term—*sanyasi*.

III

This section discusses all the results obtained earlier from the analysis of individual myths. It attempts to show that the myths, taken together, define a total universe of discourse in terms of the relations between the categories representing the asocial and social, and then, within the social, in terms of relations between categories representing the holders of temporal power, inherent spiritual merit, and others.

The various relations that we obtained from the analysis of the individual myths in Section II, can be briefly stated as follows:

(1) Brahman mediates between physical and social.

(2) (Brahman: Vanika $\simeq$ (*sanyasi*: *grihastha*).

(3) *Sanyasa* is a category which is (i) voluntaristic, and (ii) asocial in the sense of ultra-mundane.

(4) The category Vanika/Shudra is in a relation of opposition to the category *Sanyasa*.

(5) (Brahman: *sanyasi*) $\simeq$ (Inherent spiritual merit: Acquired spiritual merit) $\simeq$ (Punitive powers: Expiatory powers).

(6) King has only temporal power/Brahman has only spiritual merit inherent in his position. The relation between king and Brahman is that of exchange resulting in mutual dependence.

(7) Brahman mediates between king and gods. Brahman mediates for Vanikas/Shudras in their rites of passage.

Before going on to show how these relations define a total universe of discourse the meaning of the categories, Brahman, *sanyasi*, Vanika/ Shudra, and king, must first be discussed as it emerges from these relations. It seems that the first five myths related in Section I are mainly concerned with defining these categories and it is only when the relations emerging from these myths are taken collectively that the conceptual order of Hinduism can be established.

The category Brahman, in its most general meaning, is equivalent to mediator between the physical and the social as shown in relation (1). In relation (2), the category Brahman is opposed to the category Vanika and this opposition is established as equivalent to the opposition between *sanyasa* and *garhasthya*. From the second myth, 'The Creation of Vanikas', it is clear that the relation between Vanika and *grihastha* is that of identity since the Vanikas in the myth are described as followers of the *grihastha dharma*. From the same relation of equivalence it is clear that in relation to the category Vanika, the category Brahman is either identical with, or parallel to, *sanyasi*. However, since in relation (5), Brahman is opposed to *sanyasi*, we know that the relation between these two categories cannot be that of identity. Therefore, we conclude that the category Brahman is opposed to the category Vanika and in relation to the latter the category Brahman is parallel to the category *sanyasi*.

In relation (4), an opposition was established between the category Vanika/Shudra and *sanyasi*. From relations (2), (4), and (5), we can easily show that the category Brahman mediates between the opposite terms Vanika/Shudra and *sanyasi*. In deriving the relation of equivalence (2) in the previous section, we had shown that the relation between *grihastha* and *sanyasi* was that of antithetical binary opposition. Now, since the relation between *grihastha* and Vanika in relation (2) is that of identity, we can conclude that the relation between the category Vanika/Shudra and *sanyasi* is one of antithetical opposition. This would further mean that any other term which is also opposed to *sanyasi* will have some parallelism to the category Vanika. Now, we know from relation (5) that in some contexts the category Brahman is opposed to the category *sanyasi* and therefore we conclude the term Brahman is parallel to the term Vanika in relation to the *sanyasi*. Also, we already know that in some other contexts, the term Brahman is opposed to the term Vanika and in relation to the latter, it is parallel to the term *sanyasi*.

In fact, it may be said that in opposition to the *sanyasi*, Brahmans take on some of the characteristics of the householders within the caste system. In relation to the latter, however, Brahman comes to be vested with some characteristics of the renouncer.[1] Thus we find that the meaning of the category Brahman is not fixed but changes according to context. In fact, the category Brahman juxtaposes in itself the opposite characteristics of the Vanika/Shudra, and the *sanyasi*, since it is parallel to each of these in different contexts. It therefore appears that the category Brahman juxtaposes the characteristics of these opposite terms precisely because it mediates between them and hence has to oscillate between the two. Therefore, the category Brahman structurally mediates between the opposites Vanika/Shudra and *sanyasi*, which, as we have seen, stand for the social and asocial respectively.

In relation to the king, the Brahman acts as a mediator between him and the gods/ancestors since the sacrifice made by the king is not acceptable to them unless the Brahmans act as the officiating priests. To sum up, the principal meanings of the category Brahman are:

---

[1] A similar conclusion has been independently reached through a different type of argument by Marriott (1973).

(1) mediators between physical and social, (2) mediators between Vanika/Shudra, which is the non-Brahman mass within the social order of *varna* and householdership, and *sanyasi*, which stands for the asocial, and (3) between king and gods/ancestors.

We have described the category *sanyasi* as a voluntaristic and an asocial category. By *sanyasa*, being a voluntaristic category, it is meant that the occupant of any status within the society is free to become a *sanyasi*, or to put the same argument negatively, no one can involuntarily be a *sanyasi*. In this sense, *sanyasa* is different from the category Brahman, in that membership of this category is not pre-determined. This does not however rule out the possibility of native theories regarding persons who are likely to be successful as *sanyasis*, either in terms of their social positions or inherent personality traits.

Secondly, we have characterized *sanyasa* as an asocial category. By asocial, it is meant that the *sanyasi* is above the structural distinctions operative within society. It is not intended to imply that 'asocial' is not itself socially defined. In fact the classic definition of a *sanyasi*, as a madman, a ghost, a child, uses all the social categories of the asocial to define the *sanyasi*. (See Ghurye, 1953.)

In relation (5), the *sanyasi* was opposed to the Brahman in terms of the different kinds of spiritual merit that they possess. The spiritual merit of the *sanyasi* was characterized as acquired and that of the Brahman as inherent. By this distinction we simply mean that the spiritual merit which the Brahman has is inherent in him by virtue of birth in a particular caste, while the *sanyasi* has to succeed in *sanyasa* in order to acquire merit. Here again the possibility of native theories about inherent personality traits in certain kinds of people which would make them more successful as *sanyasis* as against others, is not denied.

The relation between the *sanyasi* and God is also significantly different from the relation between the Brahman and God. As mentioned earlier, the *sanyasi* can *force* God to establish a relation with him if his austerity is severe enough. In fact students of Hindu mythology are familiar with the theme. The legendary Ravana had to stand on his hands for ten thousand years as austerity. But in the end he was successful in getting a boon of near immortality. The same was true of other demons, such as Hiranyakashipu. In a sense then, severe austerity is capable of bringing the gods under the power of the *sanyasi*. The Brahman, on the other hand, is not shown to command such power over gods, though his person is sacred as we shall soon show.

The Vanika/Shudra category, as pointed out in the course of the discussion in the second section, represents categories other than Brahman who are within the social order of *varna* and householdership. It is to this category that *sanyasa*, as an asocial, ultra-mundane category is essentially opposed.

The king represents temporal power. As the story of King Aama which will be analysed in the next section shows, kingship has only a partial reference to the Kshatriya category. The king, 'whether he be Kshatriya or Shudra', as the story of King Aama tells us, is defined in terms of the temporal power which he holds and in terms of his relation to the Brahman. The king has temporal power but no inherent spiritual merit. He has to depend for acquisition of spiritual merit on the mediation of the Brahman, and in return he gives temporal protection to the Brahman.

We now have the definitions of the categories essential to define the total universe of discourse. The myths start by distinguishing between the asocial and social, which are exhaustive categories and this is expressed in the opposition between *sanyasa* and Vanika/Shudra categories. The relation between institutionalized renunciation and the order of caste relations has been examined by Dumont (1960). He stresses, quite rightly, that to understand Hinduism and to reduce the diversity that one encounters in its study to some kind of unity it is essential to examine it in terms of the relations between the 'renouncer' and the 'man-in-the-world'. However, it would appear from his paper that he regards the relation between the caste-order which represents the mundane for him and asceticism which represents the negation of the world and hence the ultra-mundane, as that of an unmediated opposition.

In this context, it does seem that in fact the opposition between the asocial and social (to revert to the terminology that is being used here) is not unmediated as Dumont has supposed it to be. As already shown, it is mediated by the category Brahman. It is because Dumont has not conceived of the Brahman as a mediating category that the place assigned to the Brahman in his essay is not entirely convincing. He notes, for instance, that while institutionalized ultra-mundaneness has rightly received emphasis in studies of Hinduism, he finds it difficult to accept that this ultra-mundaneness should be directly attributed to Brahmans either explicitly or implicitly, as Albert

Schweitzer (1951) and Max Weber (1923) respectively have done. Dumont tries to refute this proposition by arguing that in fact the position of the Brahman is opposed to the position of the ascetic.

The Brahmans as priests superior to all men are comfortably enough settled in the world. On the other hand, it is well-known that whoever seeks liberation must leave the world and adopt an entirely different mode of life. This is an institution, *Samnyasa*, renunciation, in fact a social state apart from society proper. (Dumont, 1960: 44.)

However, having established an opposition between the Brahman and the ascetic, Dumont does note that Brahmanical values have a lot in common with the values of the renouncer. He attributes this to an aggregation of the renouncer's values to the religion of the Brahman. He argues that the discipline of the renouncer tolerates and accepts the religion of the man-in-the-world, and therefore, by its very tolerance, it becomes an accretion to the religion of the man-in-the-world, opening up possibilities of aggregation. Thus over time, he argues, the religion of the man-in-the-world and especially that of the Brahman combined in itself more and more the values of the *sanyasi*. In fact Dumont goes to the extent of contending that the true development of Hinduism is to be understood in the *sanyasic* developments on the one hand and their aggregation to the worldly religions on the other.

An attempt will be made to show the weakness inherent in this theory of aggregation in the next section. Here it is only necessary to point out that this explanation in terms of aggregation is inadequate in that it overlooks the unique structural position of the Brahman *vis-à-vis* the opposition between the asocial and social. Both the ultra-mundaneness attributed to the Brahman by Schweitzer and Weber on the one hand, and opposition between Brahman and ascetic demonstrated by Dumont on the other, are in fact correct, and even necessary since the category Brahman is a mediating term between the polar opposites asocial and social. Therefore it is essential that the category Brahman should subsume in itself some of the opposing characteristics of the asocial and social, which is why in some contexts it becomes similar to the *sanyasi* and in others opposed to it. In fact this ambiguity and equivocality is essential to the character of a mediating term, for, as Lévi-Strauss (1963b: 39) has noted in a different context, '. . . since his [the trickster's] mediating function occupies a position halfway between two polar terms, he must retain something of that duality—namely an ambiguous and equivocal character'.

Similarly, the apparently anomalous character of the category Brahman results from the structural position of this category in the conceptual framework of Hinduism, and not because the structure is 'blurred and indistinct' at the Sanskritic level (Dumont, 1960: 42). Thus, while it is true that historically the Brahman has appropriated many of the values of the *sanyasi*, such as vegetarianism and emphasis on non-violence, it is precisely the structural position of the Brahman which allows him to appropriate the values of the *sanyasi*. In this context then it becomes possible to explain both structure and process within the same framework of analysis.

Having examined the opposition between the asocial and social and shown that it is, in fact, a mediated opposition, let us proceed to a discussion of the categories necessary to define the social and the relations between these categories. The three categories which exhaust the universe of the social, in this argument, are Brahman, king and others, the last being a general category to define the non-Brahman mass within the social order of caste and householdership and represented in the myths by the Vanika/Shudra category. The Brahman, as will be obvious by now, is defined as social in some contexts and asocial in others.

The conception of kingship and the relation between king and Brahman in ancient India has been very lucidly discussed by Dumont (1962). Following Hocart (1969) he has pointed out that in most societies where kingship is found (for instance, ancient Egypt or China) it includes in itself political as well as magico-religious functions. However, these functions have been split in ancient India so that the king has only naked power while the Brahman has spiritual merit. He further demonstrates that king can never subsume the function of Brahman, while Brahman can never usurp power. So far, the relations (1) and (7) obtained from the myth, 'The Sorrows of Shrimata', support Dumont's contention. The myth further establishes a relation of exchange between the king and the Brahman—the king acquiring spiritual merit through the mediation of the Brahman and giving temporal protection to him in exchange. Thus a relation of mutual dependence is established between them.

So far the myth supports Dumont's contention, though in the next part of the argument there are some serious modifications to be offered. While Dumont is essentially correct in characterizing the relation between king and Brahman as that of mutual dependence, he contends that logically kingship includes in itself the 'magico-religious functions' and the 'political functions', and that in the case of India king becomes *secularized*, passing on the magico-religious functions to Brahman. From the myth, 'The Sorrows of Shrimata', it is clear that kingship is not conceived of as consisting of both these functions, which are later split. In fact in the first part of the myth, which would correspond to the logically prior state, it is made quite clear that though the king has temporal power he cannot perform the sacrifice except through the mediation of the Brahmans. The Brahmans, instead of taking on the magico-religious functions of the king as Dumont's argument would have us suppose, in fact refuse to perform the sacrifice since their dharma is *shilocha*, i.e. they do not accumulate food for more than one day. Clearly, in this part of the myth the Brahmans, in relation to the king, are parallel to the *sanyasi*. Their refusal to accept the gifts, which would result in accumulation, represents this parallelism.

In the second part of the myth a relation of exchange is established between the king and the Brahmans and, in the light of the analysis made in the first part, this has to be again understood with reference to the latent term *sanyasi*. By accepting the gifts of the king the relation of the Brahmans to the king becomes opposed to the relation between the *sanyasi* and the king. The former is now a relation of exchange resulting in dependence and the latter is a relation of independence *vis-à-vis* the king. Unless we bring in the latent term *sanyasi* and understand the relation between king and Brahman with reference to the relation between king and *sanyasi* it becomes difficult to explain why the Brahmans refused to officiate in the sacrifice and refused the gifts of even such a meritorious king as Rama.

This argument of the Brahmans in which they characterize themselves as people whose *dharma* is non-accumulation can be understood only if we assume the third latent term—*sanyasi*. Clearly we have here a tripartite classification with one term latent[1]—and the myth establishes the *relation between the relations* of the king and Brahman, on the one hand, and the king and *sanyasi*, on the other. Incidentally, these conclusions are not being based on an atypical theme, for myths in which Brahmans first refuse to accept the gifts of the king and then are either forced due to temporal necessities or

[1] For a similar logic of classification, see Turner (1966).

lured into accepting these gifts occur in many other caste Puranas of this region, like the Nagar Khanda, Anavila Purana, Shrimala Purana, etc.

The relation between king and the category 'others' (Vanika/Shudra) is that the latter hold rights to livelihood through favour of the king. The king, as owner of all land, gives grants to Brahmans in exchange for the spiritual merit which he acquires through them, and also settles the Vanikas and Shudras in the city to serve the Brahmans. This factor of the Vanikas and Shudras being established through favour of the king is symbolized in the myth by Rama's giving them the white sword and the yak-tail switch as signs of royal favour.

The relation between Brahmans and others who are within the social order of caste (here in the sense of *varna*) and householdership, continues to be the same as established in the first myth and in relation to this category Brahmans continue to represent a parallelism to *sanyasi*. However, one sentence in the myth seems to point to an additional function of the Brahman *vis-à-vis* the Vanika/Shudra category, and that is when Rama enjoins them to worship Brahmans on all auspicious and inauspicious occasions. Now, if one interprets the auspicious and inauspicious occasions to mean the various rites of passage in the life of an individual, like birth, marriage, death, etc., it seems probable that Brahmans also mediate in the various rites of passage of householders within the caste system. I think the notion of Brahmans as mediators in the rites of passage of householders may be applied with some success in analysing their actual position in the caste system and their structural relation with other such mediators as Barbers, who also mediate at rites of passage.

We have now defined the categories which exhaust the universe of discourse and examined their relations. We have argued that the opposition between the *sanyasi* and the Vanika/Shudra category in the myths represents the opposition between the asocial and social, and that this opposition is mediated by the category Brahman. Within the social we distinguished between the holders of temporal power and inherent spiritual merit (king and Brahman respectively) and the non-Brahman mass who are householders within the *varna* order. It is the main contention of this chapter that the smallest isolate of relations in understanding Hinduism is the relation between these four categories established in two steps. The first step consists of an understanding of the opposition between the asocial and social, and its mediation, while in the second step, the social undergoes a tripartite division and an understanding of the interrelation of each division with the other is required. It is now a commonplace in studies of mythology and kinship that a proper understanding of these systems requires that the unit of study be defined not in terms of elements but in terms of relations. It is hoped that the above formulation is one step towards understanding Hinduism in terms of a set of relations rather than in terms of an enumeration of elements and traits.

One final point has to be made before we go on to the next section. It has been contended by Weber (1923:396) and Srinivas (1952:212) that the fundamental institution on which Hinduism is based is caste and that relations between castes (both in the sense of *varna* and *jati*) are essentially hierarchical. From the myths which we have analysed in this chapter, it would appear that the only *varna* term which is essential in defining the structural order of Hinduism is the category 'Brahman'. The category 'king' has some correspondence to the category 'Kshatriya' but this is not an essential correspondence. In 'The Story of King Aama', when the Brahmans are giving an exposition of the relations between Brahman and king, they clearly say, 'Whether the king is a Kshatriya or a Shudra, it is his duty to protect the Brahmans'. Therefore the relations that have been usually described or interpreted as relations between Brahman *varna* and Kshatriya *varna* within the *varna* system are clearly a special case of the general relations between Brahman and king. Similarly, the lumping together of the Vanika (even if we take it to be equivalent to the Vaishya category) and Shudra categories suggest that this category is also not so much a *varna* category as a general non-Brahman mass, consisting of householders within the caste system who have neither temporal power nor inherent spiritual merit. The relations between these three categories define the universe of the social, and there is no indication in the myths to suggest that these relations are basically hierarchical. By this statement it is not meant that all these categories are defined as equal but that it is relations other than those of equality or inequality in terms of which these categories are described. Finally, the *varna* categories are clearly not exhaustive for they leave out the category *sanyasi*, which, as we have seen, is equally important in defining the structure of Hinduism.

IV

This section first analyses the myth, 'The Story of King Aama', and then shows that the myth deals with the negation of the ideal structural order of Hinduism[1] and thereby implicitly demonstrates it.

The theme of this story is the conversion of King Aama to a heretical sect and his refusal to protect the grants given to the Brahmans. The major part of the myth revolves around the arguments between the king and the Brahmans, and finally the Brahmans are able to give irrevocable proof of their own position thanks to divine help.

The king has two main arguments on the basis of which he justifies his decision to give patronage to the *kshapanakas* (Jain mendicants) and to withdraw the support to the Brahmans extended by earlier kings. The first argument is that in terms of personal merit the Jain renouncers are better than the Brahmans and hence eminently more suitable recipients of worship of the king. The second argument is that the grants of land and villages were given to the Brahmans by King Rama who was an ordinary mortal. Therefore, the grants given by him were peculiar to his reign and there was no obligation for subsequent kings to respect the agreement.

In terms of the king's argument the characteristics of the *kshapanakas* and Brahmans respectively are as follows:

Kshapanakas	Brahmans
(1) Attitude of non-accumulation	Attitude of greed
(2) No mastery over land	Mastery over land
(3) Mastery over senses	Slaves of sensuous pleasures
(4) Practise non-violence	Practise violence

Thus the king's first argument is based on a comparison of the personal qualities of the *kshapanakas* and the Brahmans—a comparison which shows that while the *kshapanakas* are essentially ultra-mundane, the Brahmans are as involved in mundane activities as all others within the social order and hence do not deserve to be given any respect.

The reply given to this argument by the Brahmans is significant. They do not deny any of the allegations made by the king. They

---

[1] The term Hindu does not appear in the text and instead the term Vedic *dharma* is used.

admit that they are followers of the *grihastha dharma*,[1] and as such do indulge in sensuous pleasures, claiming that for living, violence of one kind or the other is essential, and that their ownership of villages is justified since the grants were given to them by a divine personage, Rama. Their argument shows that they do not wish to establish their right to the grants of villages and land on the basis of their personal merit but on the grounds that they have to be protected by the king because he is dependent on the spiritual merit which is inherent in their position. They apply a totally different logic to the assessment of the mendicants' spiritual merit for they try to demonstrate to the king that the renouncers are to be judged by their ultra-mundane qualities and that the *kshapanakas* have in fact failed to master these qualities.

Thus the first argument of the Brahmans is that they are to be judged by the spiritual merit inherent in their position and that the logic applicable to the renouncers is not applicable to them. Secondly they try to show that the *kshapanakas* have deceived the king into thinking that they have mastered the ultra-mundane qualities by which alone a renouncer is to be judged. This brings out the different logic of assessment which is applicable to the Brahmans and re-nouncers, and partitions these two categories in structural terms.

The second argument of the king, as already mentioned, is that Rama was just another king and that there is nothing sacrosanct about the order of relations established by him. The Brahmans, on the other hand, maintain that Rama was a divine personage and that the order of relations established by him is, therefore, ideal and sacrosanct.[2] The crucial part of the argument, then, hinges on the divinity of Rama, for on that rests the proof of the ideal nature of the relations between Brahman and king, Brahman and *sanyasi*, and king and *sanyasi*.

The Brahmans are finally able to convince the king of the rightness

[1] The Brahmans are mentioned in the myth for the first time as followers of *grihastha dharma*. It is hoped that the logic of the text which is developed by defining each category in relation to other categories, will make it clear that this does not alter the parallelism of the Brahman to the *sanyasi* in relation to the Vanika.

[2] The king is represented in Sanskrit literature as the protector of both the moral and natural order. If the king is himself corrupt or if he allows the moral order to collapse, then it inevitably leads to the collapse of the natural order resulting in drought and famine. The story of King Vena, mentioned in the next chapter, shows this.

5

of the structure of relations established by Rama by getting proof of Rama's divinity through Hanumana. The proper *varnashrama-dharma* is reinstated in place of the heretic sect by the king's acknowledgment of his spiritual dependence on the Brahmans, granting them temporal protection and banishing the Jain renouncers, who preached against this structural order, from his kingdom.

It is clear from the analysis of the myth that it demonstrates the structural order of Hinduism in terms of a tripartite division of the domains of Brahman, king, and *sanyasi* which are categorically partitioned. Jainism and Buddhism (the words are used interchangeably in the myth) are precisely conceptualized as heretic sects in the myth, in that they obliterate the partitioning of these categories and they further confuse the relations of each category with the other. In the myth, when King Aama is converted to a heretic sect, he first obliterates the partitioning between the categories Brahman and *sanyasi* by applying the same logic of the assessment of spiritual merit to the Brahmans as is applicable to the renouncers. He then confuses the relations between each category as defined in the conceptual order of Hinduism. The relations between king and Brahman are confused by the refusal of King Aama to grant temporal protection to Brahmans and his denial of the king's spiritual dependence on Brahmans. Finally, King Aama gives patronage to the renouncers and makes their ethics the measuring rod of spiritual merit of any kind. Thus all three kinds of relations—that between king and Brahman, Brahman and *sanyasi*, and *sanyasi* and king—are confused and in this lies the heresy of the Jain and Buddhist sects.

In a recent paper on the five symbols of Sikhism, Uberoi (1967) has shown that the meaning of the five symbols of Sikhism, taken together, can be understood only in relation to the structural order of Hinduism. He has argued that as a social movement, Sikhism 'set out to annihilate the categorical partitions, intellectual and social, of the medieval world' (Uberoi, 1967: 98). These partitions, according to him, were the splitting up of the medieval world into a tripartite division among (1) the rulers (the world of *rajya*), (2) the caste system (*varna, grihastha*), and (3) the orders of renunciation (*sanyasa*). The final meaning of the five symbols of Sikhism, he argues, was the rejection of the opposition between these categories and the investment of the virtues of all three in a single body of faith and conduct.

It would therefore seem that the major conclusion Uberoi has reached is of tremendous value for it can be extended to include not only rebel sects other than Sikhism but also the perception in structural terms of these rebel sects by Hindu thinkers. As a general conclusion it can be stated that sects which attempted to rebel against Hindu *dharma* tried to do so by rejecting the categorical partitions obtaining in Hinduism and confusing the relations between each category as established in the structural order of Hinduism. Moreover, it appears that the perception of these sects by Hindu thinkers was not in terms of their rebellion against the caste system as has so often been assumed, but in terms of their negation of the conceptual order of Hinduism.

There is however one important modification to be made to Uberoi's thesis. He has stated that the medieval world was split into a tripartite division among the rulers, the caste system, and the orders of renunciation. We have already seen that as far as medieval Hinduism is concerned the structure of relations is in terms of an opposition between the asocial and social, and then within the social in terms of a tripartite division between king, Brahman, and non-Brahman mass of householders within the caste system who have neither temporal power nor inherent spiritual merit. In 'The Story of King Aama' it is the division in the domain of Brahman, king and *sanyasi* which suffices to define the structural order of Hinduism. Conceptually, the category of common householders within the caste system becomes latent here—a dummy in the game of three—since both the categories of Brahman and *sanyasi* were defined through the relation of opposition or parallelism to this category. This last point is important for, while in this myth the Vanika/Shudra category was latent so that the other three categories sufficed to define the structural order of Hinduism, it is expected that other myths will be found in which one of the other categories may be latent.

To return to Uberoi's argument. He has shown great insight in analysing the relation between the heterodox sects and Hinduism in terms of a grammar of structural relations. He has however simplified the nature of the categorical partitions and the structure of relations essential to define the Hinduism of the medieval period. It is hoped that the analysis of myths here has been able to demonstrate the nature of relations between the four categories which are essential in defining the structural order of Hinduism.

Incidentally, this opportunity may be taken to show the weakness in Dumont's theory of the aggregation of the renouncers' values to the values of the man-in-the-world, to explain the development of

Hinduism. In analysing the place of Tantra in Hinduism, Dumont (1960) contends that in Tantrism we find a rejection of ascetic renunciation and in its place a reversal of ordinary values. 'The rejection of asceticism is expressed in the rehabilitation of enjoyment, *bhoga*. But it is characteristic that *yoga*, or the discipline of liberation, is at the same time preserved, and that the doctrine claims to transcend the opposition of *yoga*, discipline, and *bhoga*, enjoyment.' 'Either the *yogi* is not a *bhogi* (enjoyer) or the *bhogi* knows not *yoga* [we are lost in contradiction], that is why only the *kaula* doctrine, whose essence is of *bhoga* and *yoga*, is superior to all.' (p. 53)

'We see that in rejecting renunciation, Tantrism accepts ideas deriving from it. Far from making a *tabula rasa*, it builds upon what has been acquired through renunciation and has become a sort of universal language in India.' (p. 53).

We can see clearly in these quotations that Tantrism, in fact, rejects the categorical partition between *bhoga* and *yoga* by investing their virtues conjointly in a single doctrine. Dumont is himself very near this conclusion when he states that the doctrine *claims* to transcend the opposition between *yoga* and *bhoga*. But from this claim he goes on to conclude that even in rejecting asceticism, Tantrism accepts ideas deriving from it. It is hoped that from the analysis made in this section it is sufficiently clear that Dumont's conclusion misplaces the emphasis in analysing movements like Tantrism. The important point here is not that it accepts ideas deriving from asceticism even while rejecting it, but that it rejects the categorical partition between *yoga* and *bhoga*—the values of the *sanyasi* and the values of the man-in-the-world—and therefore negates the grammar of structural relations in Hinduism. Thus its structural position is similar to that of other heterodox sects which have been analysed earlier.

3
Of Jatis

I

In the last chapter the myths in the Dharmaranya Purana which were relevant for an understanding of the categories Brahman, *sanyasi*, and king were analysed. On the basis of these myths, the conceptual order of Hinduism in terms of a set of relations among these categories was constructed. This chapter will be devoted to an analysis of the myths which relate to differentiation among the Brahmans and Vanikas. We hope to demonstrate on the basis of these myths that *jatis* are placed in the conceptual order of Hinduism, not with reference to other like units but with reference to the set of relations among Brahman, king, and *sanyasi*, established earlier. It shall be further shown that a *jati* is identified by a combination of three principles of organization, viz. descent, locality, and cult. Finally it appears from the myths that the language in which the relationship between castes is expressed is the language of exchange; elaborate rules being prescribed placing limits to circulation of food, goods and services, and women. There are, then, three separate universes of discourse: (a) the tripartite classification of Brahman, king, and *sanyasi*, (b) the identification of descent, locality and cult-group as principles of organization, and (c) rules determining the limits to exchange of food, goods and services, and women. These operate at different levels defining respectively the conceptual order of Hinduism, the identification of *jatis* in Hinduism and the relations between different *jatis* at the empirical level as perceived by Puranic thinkers.

II

This section relates the main divisions among the Brahmans that are described and the reasons given in the Purana for the divisions that took place. As noted in the last chapter, the creation of the Brahmans differentiated physical space from social space. With the creation of the Vanikas/Shudras, Brahmans were differentiated from the other categories of people. Then, within the Brahman grouping, the Modh Brahmans were distinguished from other Brahmans on the basis of locality. Among the Modh Brahman grouping, the two categories, Trivedi Modhs and Chaturvedi Modhs, were distinguished. The Trivedi Modhs were further subdivided into the Dhenujas and other Trivedis, while the Chaturvedis had four divisions—Mallas, Tanduliyas, an unnamed group of 111 Chaturvedis and the remaining Chaturvedis.

A chart below shows the major divisions and sub-divisions among the Brahmans, as represented in the Dharmaranya Purana.

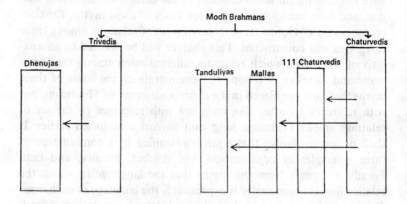

We shall now recount the principal events which, according to the Purana, are responsible for the divisions among the Brahmans. The Brahmans are spoken of as a composite category till the myth, 'The Sorrows of Shrimata'. In this myth, the word Modh was prefixed to the word Brahmans for the first time in the Purana, when Rama spoke of them as Modh Brahmans, meaning Brahmans from Modhera. Thus the Brahmans of the locality were implicitly distinguished from the Brahmans of other localities.

It was also in this myth that the Modh Brahmans were categorized as either Trivedis or Chaturvedis. The Trivedis were those Modh Brahmans who agreed to perform the fire-sacrifice for Rama and accepted *dakshina* (fee for the officiating priest) and *dana* (gifts of charity) from him. The Chaturvedis were those Modh Brahmans who refused to perform the sacrifice or accept gifts from Rama, even at the exhortation of the gods. However, temporal necessities later forced them to accept the grants given by Rama, and on his second visit to Moheraka they performed the fire-sacrifice for him. Thus the initial reason for which the Brahmans were divided disappeared since both divisions accepted the gifts of Rama.[1] However, the two different categories continued to be designated by separate names and it is to be noted that the two divisions were settled in separate places by Rama—the Trivedis in Moheraka and the Chaturvedis in Sitapura.

Further differences arose between the Trivedis and the Chaturvedis in 'The Story of King Aama', which was given in the last chapter. According to this story, King Aama refused to recognize the grants given to the Brahmans by Rama. When the Brahmans argued that Rama was a divine personage and therefore the grants given by him should be given due recognition, the king demanded concrete proof of Rama's divinity. He asked the Brahmans to produce Hanumana in person in his court since Rama had entrusted them to Hanumana's care.

Now differences arose between the Trivedis and the Chaturvedis on the advisability of trying to propitiate Hanumana through severe penance, in order that he might appear to the Brahmans in person. The Trivedis argued that it was the duty of the Brahmans to protect their *vritti* (grants, source of livelihood). Therefore, they further argued, they should make every attempt to please Hanumana who would be able to suggest the proof that should be given of Rama's divinity to King Aama. The Trivedis argued that this was the only way in which they would be able to protect their *vritti*. The Chaturvedis, on the other hand, argued that it would be impossible for the Brahmans to see Hanumana in person and obtain a proof of Rama's divinity that would satisfy King Aama. Therefore they thought it more advisable for the Brahmans to take up the source of livelihood of the Vanikas.

After much argument, the Chaturvedis were finally persuaded by the Trivedis to follow the course of action proposed by them. The Trivedis and Chaturvedis selected their representatives who proceeded to the forest in order to propitiate Hanumana through severe austerity. However, the representatives sent by the Chaturvedis were fickle-minded. They were unable to bear the hazards of the journey to the forest and therefore returned without having accomplished

[1] The only exception was the group of 111 Chaturvedis who refused to accept the gifts of Rama even at the exhortation of the three gods.

their mission. The Trivedis, on the other hand, managed to propitiate Hanumana who was so pleased by their devotion and severe austerities that he appeared to them in person. Hanumana gave them the hair from his right and left sides and told them how it would convince King Aama of Rama's divinity (see p. 31). The Brahmans went, armed with the two parcels of hair given by Hanumana, to King Aama. The king disbelieved their story initially, but when his palace and army started burning because of the curse put on them by the Brahmans in accordance with Hanumana's instructions, he acknowledged the divinity of Rama and reinstated the grants given to the Brahmans.

Thus both the Trivedi and Chaturvedi Modhs got back the grants. The king settled the two groups in different places—the Trivedis in Dharmaranya and the Chaturvedis in Sukhavasapura. However, because the Chaturvedis had refused to co-operate with the Trivedis in their efforts to propitiate Hanumana, the Trivedis broke off relations of marriage with them and the two groups were separated from each other.

Thus the reasons for the divisions among the Brahmans in terms of Modh Brahmans and other Brahmans, and the further divisions of the Modh Brahmans into Trivedis and Chaturvedis, can be abstracted from the myths, 'The Sorrows of Shrimata' and 'The Story of King Aama', which were related in the previous chapter. The Purana also has two separate chapters devoted to an account of the 'caste' (i.e. *jati*) and 'territorial' divisions among the Trivedi and Chaturvedi Modhs. The gist of these two chapters is given below.

It will be recalled that the Chaturvedis were divided into four separate groups—the Mallas, Tanduliyas, an unnamed division of 111 Chaturvedis, and the other Chaturvedis. According to the Dharmaranya Purana, the Chaturvedis had sent twenty Brahmans as their representatives who went with the representatives of the Trivedis to the forest in order to propitiate Hanumana. Now these twenty Brahmans discontinued the journey due to the hazards which they had to face in the forest. Of these twenty there were some Brahmans who did not return to Modhera but settled down in foreign countries (i.e. places other than Modhera which is in North Gujarat). They were good at fighting with their hands and so became wrestlers and were known as Mallas. Not only did they settle in 'foreign' places but also wore clothes which made them difficult to identify and had promiscuous relations with wives of other men. These Brahmans formed a separate division. They married among themselves and their *kuladevi* (goddess of the lineage) was the Shakti goddess Nimbaja.

Of these twenty Chaturvedis who were returning from the forest, there were some Brahmans who settled down in a place called Tandula. They adopted the occupations of Vaishyas. They also formed a separate division and came to be known as 'Tanduliyas'— after the place in which they had settled. Their *kuladevi* was the Vaishnavi goddess Paramaranda.

The unnamed division of the 111 Chaturvedis was formed by those Chaturvedi Brahmans who had refused to accept the grants given by Rama even on his second visit when the other Chaturvedis had all agreed to accept them. These 111 Chaturvedis subsisted by practising the occupation of Vanikas. Thus their different occupation and residence caused them also to form a separate division. Their *kuladevi* was the beautiful Shakti goddess called Chhatra.

The rest of the Chaturvedi Brahmans were busy in *karmakanda* (performance of ceremonies). They stayed in the villages by the bank of the Sabarmati river where they were established by the king. The Suta concludes by saying that 'whatever caste (*jati*) and territorial differences arose among the Chaturvedi Brahmans have been related by me'.

After this the division among the Trivedis, into Dhenujas and other Trivedis, is accounted for by the following tale.

The Trivedi Brahmans had many cows and they employed some young men to take these cows for grazing. The boys used to take the cows for grazing near the Gambhira river from sunrise to sunset. Some widows and unmarried girls used to take food and water for these boys. The boys would bathe in the river and then eat the food brought to them by the girls.

Thus time passed and slowly a sense of familiarity developed between the boys and girls. The boys became desirous of the girls and after a time they became lovers. The parents of the girls had no knowledge of this. After some months had elapsed, the girls and the widows became pregnant and their elders learnt about the whole affair. Then the elders called all the Brahmans who assembled together to decide the further course of action. The assembly of Brahmans scanned the Dharmashastras and decided that the girls had been polluted and hence they and their future children had to be separated from the other Brahmans. They said, 'These girls have been polluted. From them will be born children such as *kanina* and *golaka*.[1] We must act according to the Dharmashastras so that no mixture of *varnas* [*varna-samkara*] results. These girls and widows should be married to the boys. The boys have lost their *dharma*. So let them become *grihasthas*. These low Brahmans will be known as Dhenujas. Their *jati* is different. We shall have no relations with them. Other people will know them as Dhenuja Modhs.'

Then the Brahmans married off the girls to the boys, gave them clothes and ornaments, and sent them away to a town called Dhenuja where they were settled. These Dhenujas were also known as Modh Brahmans. However, they had no relations with the other Trivedi Brahmans and formed a separate division. Their *kuladevi* was the Shakti goddess called Bhadrika.

III

After discussing the differences that arose among the Trivedi and Chaturvedi Brahmans, there is a narration of how the Modh Brahmans established a code of conduct to protect their *dharma* in the Kaliyuga. Since this narration is extremely useful in decoding the language in which relationships between *jatis* are expressed, it is being reproduced here in its entirety. It has been thought necessary to adhere as closely as possible to the Sanskrit idiom.

Once all the Brahmans of Modhera met and decided that a new code of conduct had to be established so that they might be able to protect their *dharma* in the sinful Kaliyuga. They all decided to observe the following restrictions.

First of all, it was decided that *yajnas* for lower *varnas* would not be performed by the Brahmans and no gifts were to be accepted from members of these *varnas*. The *varnas* which were considered to be lower were Washermen, Leather-workers, Dancers, Drummers, Fishermen, and Bhils. The Brahmans were forbidden from accepting any gifts from members of these *varnas*. Whoever accepted gifts from them was to be known as belonging to a lowly house, the

[1] The *kanina* and *golaka* categories refer to children who are born out of wedlock and are to be treated as Shudras. They are different from children born to women who are married from genitors other than their husbands. The latter custom was known as *niyoga* and was allowed by the Dharmashastras. (Kane, 1941, vol. II: 54)

polluter of the *pankti* (line),[1] and was to be avoided by all others.

It was decided that the Brahman who did not take the ritual bath and say his evening prayers would have to undergo *prayaschita* (act of religious atonement) in accordance with procedures prescribed by the Dharmashastras. Any Brahman who renounced the Vedic religion and became a follower of the heretic religions was to be avoided by all since he was a denouncer of the Vedic *dharma*. No one was to accept the food of any Brahman who did not make oblations to ancestors in the prescribed period. Finally, any Brahman who infringed these rules was to be known as the polluter of the caste. No other Brahman was to be allowed to eat with such a person, and anyone who accepted food from him was to be punished. Earlier the rule had been that food could be accepted from the house in which a daughter had been given in marriage. This rule was not to be followed in Kaliyuga. In earlier ages it had been permissible for the different *jatis* to eat together. Though the Dharmashastras did not say that there was any difference, yet the different *jatis* of the Brahmans were in future not to accept food from each other.

Manu and other authors who had codified the religious laws had permitted the acceptance of wives from the lower *varnas*. However, in the Kaliyuga the Brahmans were not to be permitted to accept wives from the lower *varnas*. These new rules which restricted the acceptance of food and wives from other *jatis* were to be strictly followed by the residents of Dharmaranya.

The Brahmans further ruled that whoever accepted money for giving his daughter in marriage was to be regarded as someone who had sold his daughter. Such a person was to be universally avoided. Also, any Brahman who did not worship the goddess Matangi during the weddings was to be carefully avoided by everyone.

If a Brahman committed a murder, then he was to perform the requisite act of penance in accordance with the procedures laid down in the Dharmashastras. If a Brahman, a woman, a child, or a cow had been killed, then a *vrata* for the duration of twelve years would have to be performed. Drinking liquor was to be regarded as sinful as killing and accordingly punished.

A Brahman who desired his preceptor's wife was to be severely punished. A Brahman who took a wife from another *jati* was to be

---

[1] *Pankti* refers to the line in which people sit when they are served with food on ritual occasions, such as marriage feasts or feasts given at funerals. Ordinarily only people of the same caste can sit in the same *pankti*. (See Mayer, 1960: 33.)

avoided like a Shudra, but no punishment was to be prescribed for him.

A Brahman who adopted the Jain *dharma* due to greed or ignorance, or took refuge in the Bauddha *dharma*, was to be considered as a denouncer of the Vedic religion and accordingly punished. He would be required to perform the act of penance in accordance with procedures laid down in the Dharmashastras.

In a subsequent chapter, the Suta describes the decline of Dharmaranya towards the end of Kaliyuga. According to these predictions, when the end of Kaliyuga arrived the Brahmans would not remain the repositories of Vedic learning. They would be ill, avaricious, would not perform the daily cleansing rituals and would be like Shudras. They would become subservient to the Shudras and would accept the task of performing household duties. In Dharmaranya there would be an abundance of thieves and Bhils.

Vanikas would not serve Brahmans and would accept the source of livelihood of Vaishyas. They would roam around from place to place in order to earn money. Vanikas would be full of arrogance while Brahmans would have no grants of land and villages. They would be tortured by the Mlecha kings. Poor Brahmans would have to serve Shudras. They would have no knowledge of the Vedas and would even sell their daughters. In this period, the importance of pilgrimages would decline and it was only with the coming of the Kritayuga again that Dharmaranya would regain its lost importance.

IV

This section analyses the Puranic thinkers' description of the differences among the Brahmans. It is hoped that this analysis will throw light on the concept of *jati* and its meaning and place in the conceptual orders of Hinduism.

One of the differences between the *varna* scheme and the 'ethnographical reality' of caste is that while according to the *varna* scheme there are only four castes, the number of castes in existence (i.e. *jatis*) has been calculated in most linguistic regions to be around 3000. Thus Srinivas (1962) has pointed out,

Firstly, according to the *varna* scheme there are only four castes excluding the Untouchables, and the number is the same in every part of India. But even during Vedic times there were occupational groups which were not subsumed by *varna* even though it is not known whether such groups were castes in the sense sociologists understand the term.

However, the lack of fit between the existing *jatis* and the *varna* scheme is a theme which occurs in the writings of early Hindu thinkers. For instance, Manu tried to account for the proliferation of *jatis* by his theory of *varna-samkara*, according to which the inter-*varna* marriages resulted in the formation of *jatis* which could not be given a place in the *varna* scheme.[1] It is obvious that Manu's theory cannot adequately explain the vast number of *jatis* which find no place in the *varna* scheme. But the point is that Hindu thinkers were themselves aware that the *jatis* were anomalous in relation to the *varna* order. Therefore it is interesting to see the logic by which the 'fission' of castes is explained in this Purana and the light that this sheds on the conception of a *jati*.

We shall begin with the division of the Modh Brahmans into the Trivedis and Chaturvedis. In order to facilitate the analysis, all the statements made about the differences between Trivedis and Chaturvedis are presented as follows:

Trivedis	*Chaturvedis*
1 They performed a sacrifice for Rama and accepted *dakshina* (gifts for the officiating priests) and *dana* (gifts of charity) from him.	Initially they refused to either accept gifts from Rama or perform the sacrifice for him.
2 When King Aama demanded proof of Rama's divinity, they (the Trivedis) argued in favour of going to the forest and pleasing Hanumana through severe austerities as it was the duty of Brahmans to protect their *vritti*.	The Chaturvedis argued that it would be better for the Brahmans to take up the *vritti* of the Vanikas instead of trying to protect their own *vritti*. However, they were finally persuaded to take up the course of action proposed by the Trivedis.
3 The Trivedis succeeded in pleasing Hanumana with their severe austerities and devotion. They obtained proof of Rama's divinity from Hanumana and thus convinced King Aama of their right to temporal protection from him.	The representatives of the Chaturvedis returned from the forest without having secured proof of Rama's divinity.

(Continued)

---

[1] For an account of Manu's theory of *varna-samkara* see Kane (1941, vol. II: 1). In this context, see the recent note by Sharma (1975).

Trivedis	Chaturvedis
1a The *gotras*, *prayaras*, and *attankas* (surnames) of the Trivedis were different from those of the Chaturvedis.[1]	The *gotras*, *pravaras*, and *attankas* of the Chaturvedis were different from those of the Trivedis.
2a The Trivedis stayed in Dharmaranya.	The Chaturvedis were settled in Sitapura, Sukhavasapura and in the villages along the Sabarmati river.
3a The Trivedis performed the *shrauta karma*, i.e. the performance of elaborate Vedic sacrificial rituals which were not specific to the domestic group.	The Chaturvedis performed the *karmakanda*, i.e. the performance of domestic rituals.

It will be quite clear that the first three statements try to give *explanations* of why the Trivedis became differentiated from the Chaturvedis, while the last three statements simply give certain diacritical marks with the help of which the two divisions are identified.

In the first statement, the Trivedis are distinguished from the Chaturvedis in terms of their relation to King Rama. As will be clear from the detailed analysis of the myth, 'The Sorrows of Shrimata', in Chapter 2, the performance of the sacrifices for Rama by the Trivedis symbolizes a relation of exchange between Brahman and king, resulting in their mutual dependence. In this context, the refusal of the Chaturvedis to perform the sacrifice for Rama and accept gifts from him symbolizes their independence *vis-à-vis* the king. It is true that these differences later disappear because the Chaturvedis are forced to perform a sacrifice for Rama and accept his gifts because of temporal exigencies, but the important point is that *the differences between the Trivedis and Chaturvedis are conceptualized in the myths of the Dharmaranya Purana, with reference to the relation of each division to the king.*

Subsequent differences that arose among the Trivedis and Chaturvedis are expounded in 'The Story of King Aama' and are summarized in statements 2 and 3.

In statement 2, the Trivedis are distinguished from the Chaturvedis in terms of the different arguments that members of the two groups

---

[1] *Gotras* refer to loose groupings of descent among the Brahmans which trace nominal descent from ancient sages. *Pravara* is any noble ancestor who contributed to the credit of a *gotra*.

use on the question of propitiating Hanumana through severe austerities. The Trivedis argued that they would be able to propitiate Hanumana and secure the proof of Rama's divinity which would persuade King Aama to recognize their grants. The Chaturvedis, on the other hand, argued for taking up the source of livelihood of the Vanikas. We know from our analysis of this myth ('The Story of King Aama') in Chapter 2 that the divinity of Rama stands for the sacrosanctity of the order of relations among Brahman, king, and sanyasi, established by Rama which King Aama was trying to negate. In this context, the decision of the Trivedis to obtain proof of Rama's divinity stands for their resolution to protect this particular structure of relations which they consider basic to the Vedic dharma. The argument of the Chaturvedis, that they should let the king withdraw the grants and the Brahmans should adopt the occupation of the Vanikas, amounts to their readiness to give up their place in this scheme of relations. Since Brahmans were defined in a relation of opposition to the Vanika/Shudra category and since this opposition was based among other things on their opposite relations to property, it is clear that Brahmans who adopted the occupation of the Vanikas would not be in opposition to the Vanika/Shudra category. This would also mean that the relations in terms of which the category Brahman was defined (i.e. relation of exchange with the king, opposition to Vanika/Shudra category, and mediators between householders within the caste system and renouncers) would be negated. Hence, the Purana conceptualizes the difference between the two divisions of the Modh Brahmans in terms of their place in the conceptual order of Hinduism. The Trivedis adhere to the relations defined above, while the proposed resolution of the Chaturvedis amounts to the negation of these relations.

Finally, the Trivedis succeeded in their mission and obtained proof of Rama's divinity, thus convincing King Aama of his spiritual dependence on the Brahmans and their right to temporal protection from him. The Chaturvedis returned without securing proof of Rama's divinity and though they were given separate grants through the generosity of King Aama, the Trivedis refused to have any further relations of marriage with them. Thus the two divisions were wholly separated from each other.

The analysis of the explanation of the differences between Trivedis and Chaturvedis in the myth points to the conclusion that differences between these two *jatis* are explained with reference to their position in the conceptual order of Hinduism. Thus each unit is taken up and placed in relation to the king, this relation itself having been defined in the context of a set of relations between the categories Brahman, king, and *sanyasi*. At this level, the myth does not place the Trivedis or Chaturvedis in relation to other like *jatis* in a linear hierarchy but gives them a place in the more complex conceptual scheme formulated above.

The following visual representations would perhaps clarify the argument:

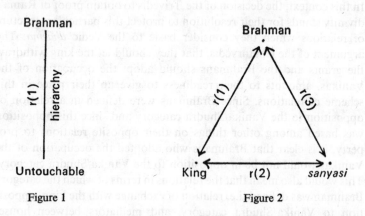

Figure 1   Figure 2

In sociological literature on Hinduism, authors such as Weber (Gerth & Mills, 1948: 396) and Srinivas (1952: 12) have assumed that (i) caste is the fundamental institution of Hinduism, and (ii) relations between castes are essentially hierarchical. They have, therefore, tended to think of the conceptual order of Hinduism as it is represented in Figure 1. In other words, in their scheme of analysis, the units are castes and the relation between these units is that of hierarchy, with Brahmans at the top and Untouchables at the bottom. This is undoubtedly an oversimplification of their views. Srinivas, for instance, introduces many more complexities in his scheme when he comes to the analysis of the middle rungs of the hierarchy. However, the representation in Figure 1 will suffice for the essential point that we wish to make, viz. that in this scheme of analysis, fission of castes is related to considerations of mobility. Thus, fission of castes occurs for a variety of reasons, such as occupational diversification, and is usually accompanied by mobility of the unit released by fission. When translated in terms of the ideas of the people regarding fission of castes it would mean that fission of castes is understood in the context of caste hierarchy, and the units released by fission are defined with references to like units in a hierarchical order.

In the conceptual scheme that emerged from analysis of the myths in Chapter 2 and represented in Figure 2, it is the partition between the categories of Brahman, king, and *sanyasi* (with the category Vanika/Shudra being latent) and the three separate kinds of relations between each of these categories, that define the conceptual order of Hinduism. At this level, therefore, the empirical units, i.e. *jatis*, are not placed in a linear hierarchical order with reference to other like units, but are placed in a triangle defined by the three respective relations between each of the categories, Brahman, king, and *sanyasi*. The importance of the principle of hierarchy in Hinduism is not being denied but we hope to show the exact level at which hierarchy becomes important as a principle of organization a little later. At this stage we hope it is sufficiently clear that the myths start at a level of abstraction at which the different kinds of relations between the categories Brahman, king, and *sanyasi* define the conceptual order of Hinduism. Then the empirical groups such as Trivedis and Chaturvedis are placed in this conceptual scheme and what constitutes an *explanation* of their differences in the myths is not their hierarchical position *vis-à-vis* each other but their respective places in this conceptual scheme.

The essential point being made here is that differences between *jatis* is not conceived in these texts as a difference of the degree of 'purity' that each *jati* has. Each *jati* is conceptualized with reference to the relations between three separate poles and is thus defined in a scheme of tripartite classification. Clearly this conception of *jatis* is more complex than a linear classification with Brahmans at one end and Untouchables on the other.

The second point that is suggested is that since *jatis* are not defined in relation to each other, it seems likely that the difference in *jatis* is not seen as one of degree but of quality. This conclusion would be supported from other sources. Thus Yalman (1963: 40) has observed in a different context, 'In fact, the informants tend to think of caste as a ritual *quality* that one has received from past generations . . . ' (emphasis supplied). Finally, it is suggested that the conceptualization of *jatis* in this manner would account for the remarkable facility with which castes who occupy a very low position in the *varna* hierarchy, like the Shudras, find it possible to subsume political power and legitimize their positions. Since the king in the conceptual scheme of Hinduism is defined by the temporal power he holds and his dependence on the spiritual merit of the Brahmans, the position of the *jatis* which are subsumed under the Shudra *varna* can be defined by a process of analogy as similar to the king if they are able to persuade Brahmans to mediate in their rites for them. In fact, in 'The Story of King Aama', the king says, 'without a part of Vishnu in him, none can become a king', an ingenious way of saying that anyone who has become a king has to have a part of Vishnu in him. Similarly, the Brahmans in this myth make no difference between kings who are Kshatriyas or Shudras, as long as they acknowledge their spiritual dependence on the Brahmans. Thus the process of the acquisition of political power by members of Shudra *varna* and the manner in which this power is legitimized, which has been widespread and regarded as an exception to the ideals of Hindu *dharma*,[1] can in fact be easily explained by taking into account this particular conceptualization of *jatis* that has been abstracted from the Dharmaranya Purana.

In the schematic representation made about Trivedis and Chaturvedis respectively in the myths (pp. 65–6), the statements 1a, 2a, and 3a refer to the different *gotras, pravaras,* and *attankas* (surnames) of the two divisions, the different localities in which they are settled, and the different cult groups (performers of *shrauta karma* and performers of *karmakanda*), to which the two divisions belong. The myths are clearly using the principles of descent, locality and cult-membership in combination as a means of identifying the Trivedis and Chaturvedis respectively. It is important to remember here that though different divisions are always identified with membership of different descent-groups, locality and cult-groups, these differences never constitute an explanation of the fission of castes in the myths. In other words, we do not find any statement in the myths which gives the *reason* for the differences between Trivedis and Chaturvedis in terms of their belonging to different descent groups, localities or cult groups. In fact, the myths always start by explaining their differences in terms of their position in the conceptual scheme

[1] For instance, Panikkar (1955) points out the unusually large number of royal families which the Shudras have produced. Srinivas also mentions that the Shudra category has been a fertile source for the recruitment of local Kshatriya and Vaishya castes, and uses this to demonstrate the distortion of empirical facts by the *varna* model.

of Hinduism, and then these differences are translated into separate diacritical marks of each group. In the 'Story of King Aama', marriage relations are broken off between the Trivedis and Chaturvedis, they are settled in different places by the king and while the former perform the *shrauta karma* the latter perform the *karmakanda*. Thus the boundaries of each group are expressed through endogamy, residence in different localities and membership of different cult-groups. We now have a second universe of discourse relating to certain principles of organization (viz. descent, locality, and cult-groups), which is used for the identification of the *jatis*. The importance of all these three principles of organization in Hinduism will be shown by defining not only *jatis* but later also deities.

After differentiating between the Trivedis and Chaturvedis, the Purana further differentiates the distinct named groups within each of these divisions. However, in order to understand the principles of differentiation at this level, it is first essential to analyse the chapter entitled 'Kalidharma-varnana' which has an elaborate exposition on the *dharma* to be followed in Kaliyuga. This material will, therefore, be analysed here and the conclusions obtained from the analysis will be used in understanding the differentiation within the Trivedi and Chaturvedi groupings respectively.

V

The theory of *kalivarjya* or things prohibited in Kaliyuga, even though they are allowed in the scriptures for other *yugas* (ages), is well known. This part of the Dharmaranya Purana is concerned with the same general theme. In it, certain prohibitions regarding marriage, commensal relations and the rendering of ritual services are advocated, though these restrictions, as the author of the Purana notes, have no basis in the Dharmashastras. It is emphasized that these restrictions become operative only in the Kaliyuga for the protection of *dharma*.

The restrictions regarding marriage are:

(1) The rules regarding acceptance of brides from other *varnas* prescribed by Manu were to be discontinued, i.e. *anuloma* marriages in which Brahmans could accept brides from other *varnas* were not to be permitted in Kaliyuga.

(2) Money for giving a daughter in marriage was not to be accepted.

(3) Preference was to be given to taking brides from one's own *jati*

and though no punishment was to be prescribed for the person who did not do so, he was to be avoided like a Shudra.

The restrictions regarding food are:

(1) While in the earlier ages it had been permissible for members of different *jatis* to eat together, this rule was to be discontinued in the Kaliyuga.

(2) Earlier, food could be accepted from the house in which a daughter had been given in marriage, but this practice also was to be discontinued.

(3) Drinking was to be considered sinful and no food was to be accepted from one who indulged in it.

(4) Food was not to be accepted from those who did not perform certain rituals like the worship of Goddess Matangi during weddings. It was also not to be accepted from those who became followers of Jain or Bauddha *dharma* and those who polluted the *pankti* (line) by breaking any of the rules laid down about marriage, commensal relations and rendering of ritual services.

The restrictions regarding the rendering of ritual services (i.e. performance of *yajnas*) were that in Kaliyuga no Brahman would perform sacrifices for the 'lower *varnas*'. The following were characterized as 'lower *varnas*' for this purpose—Washermen, Leatherworkers, Dancers, Musicians, Fishermen, and Bhilas.[1]

It is clear that certain rules are being prescribed here regarding the exchange of food, women, and services. These three items, taken

[1] It is interesting to note that the Bhilas, a tribal group, are assimilated as a category of Sanskritic civilization. They are called a *varna* here; later a story is related in which it is explained that the Bhila chieftain had been born of the left hand of a particular king Vena while a Kshatriya king Prithu was born from his right hand. The Bhila is said to have been dark, short, with yellow eyes and looked like a thief. Prithu, the Kshatriya king, is said to have been like an incarnation of God. The Bhila was given the mountains and the forests to rule over, while Prithu was given the rest of the world. We shall be analysing the symbols of laterality in the next chapter. However, it may be pointed out that Hertz (1960) has shown that the right side is associated in many parts of the world with benevolent and good-sacred forces whereas the left side is associated with malevolent and evil forces. The story seems to invest the tribal chieftain with dark and evil forces and the Hindu king with the benevolent aspects. Hocart (1969) has shown how kingship conjoins in itself justice and evil. Here the split of these two aspects between the Bhila and the Kshatriya king allows the Hindu king to become completely benevolent. Another point which may be briefly mentioned is that the category of tribe is assimilated as a category of Indian civilization. This point merits further attention from anthropologists.

together, can be regarded as prestations and, as in all societies, elaborate rules are being prescribed here regarding the categories of
people to whom these prestations can be made.

The rules regarding marriage, i.e. exchange (circulation) of women,
are expressive of extreme separation of *jatis* and prohibition of hypogamy. The rules (1) and (3), which forbid men to take brides from
other *jatis*, clearly express separation and maximum distance between
jatis. The second rule forbids the Brahmans to accept money for their
daughters in marriage. The meaning of this rule in the context of the
two earlier rules emphasizing separation between *jatis* can be understood only if we know the symbolic meaning of bride-price in the
caste system. In a very interesting study of the symbols of caste in
Ceylon (Sri Lanka) Yalman (1968) has analysed the symbolic meaning
of endogamy and hypergamy and the reasons why there is a universal
prohibition on hypogamy in the caste system. Yalman has noted that
ideally there should be no give and take of women between castes.
When there is give and take, it should be asymmetrical so that men
of high status may take women of low status but not the reverse.
Commenting on the relation between hypergamy and dowry, Yalman
(1971: 49) notes that

... in many villages [in Ceylon] there are no payments upon marriage
between equals. But it is noteworthy that when there are differences,
the women move up the hierarchy with the aid of money. Giving a
woman to someone down the hierarchy [which could be associated
with bride-wealth] would run against the grain of the symbolic system
of status definitions described above.

The link between hypergamy and dowry, and hypogamy and bride-
price in the caste system has been noted by authors other than
Yalman. Therefore we can safely conclude that the second rule which
forbids Brahmans to accept bride-price for their daughters assumes
a system of hierarchical divisions in which it is forbidden to give a
woman to someone down the hierarchy. Therefore we find that in
the rules regarding exchange of women, endogamy of *jatis* is strongly
advocated. However, breach of this rule is tolerated if the *jati* to
whom a daughter is given is equal. But accepting a 'price' for one's
daughter which would be associated with hypogamy is strictly
forbidden.

The symbolic meaning of hypogamy and its implications in the
caste system have also been very lucidly explained by Yalman (1964),
in his essay 'On the Purity of Women in the Castes of Ceylon and

Malabar'. He has argued that in castes of Ceylon and Malabar, the 'purity' of the caste community is ensured and preserved through women so that there is a great concern in ritualizing female sexuality and ensuring that low quality blood does not enter the caste through men of lower caste. Thus endogamy would result in preservation of the purity of the caste since both men and women who marry would ensure that the women would receive the male semen of a higher ritual quality so that the caste would not become polluted. But strict prohibition on hypogamy would be necessary to preserve the purity of women and through them the purity of the caste. Thus the principles of separation, ranking, and purity-pollution explain the rules regarding the exchange of women.

The restrictions regarding food refer, first, to separation. Thus acceptance of food is restricted to one's own *jati* and reaffirms the separation and distance between *jatis* expressed in rules regarding the exchange of women. The second category of people with whom eating is forbidden are those who have polluted themselves through non-observance of rituals, membership of heretical sects, or by breaking rules which have been prescribed regarding the exchange of food, women, and ritual services. This restriction combines in itself the two principles of purity-pollution and separation. Those who 'eat together' must be of the same ritual status. Therefore, those who are polluted must be separated from others who are pure in relation to them. Thus in the restrictions regarding exchange of women and food, we find all three principles, viz. separation, ranking, and purity-pollution, which have been regarded as essential in governing the relations between different castes.

The restrictions regarding the performance of *yajnas* is based on the principle of purity-pollution. The performance of *yajnas* obviously refers to the rendering of ritual and not economic services. In fact, the rendering of services in the caste system, which has been analysed from Wiser onwards in the context of the *jajmani* system, is recognized to have an important ritual context. Pocock (1962), for instance, has pointed out that the *jajmani* system subsumes in itself three different kinds of categories of clients who provide services. The first category is of those specialists whose 'specialization derives from the exigencies of the caste system and not from economic needs or from the intricacy of a craft'. In this first category he includes Barbers and Washermen, whose primary function, according to him, is to purify their higher caste patrons by removing the pollution incurred from bodily processes, and it is for this category that he would reserve the term *jajmani*. The second category is of those specialists who provide primarily economic goods or services, and the third category comprises landless labourers and is an open category, in that recruitment is not limited to a single caste. It is obvious that the services referred to in the Dharmaranya Purana are of the first kind and that the performance of rituals by the Brahman for his patrons also derives from the exigencies of the caste system. In this context Dumont (1966) has also remarked that in *jajmani* relations the ritual aspect 'encompasses' the economic aspect. It is important to stress this point because in the Purana the exchange of services is clearly linked with the exchange of food and women, and the link can only be understood if we assume that the restrictions refer to the ritual aspect of the exchange of services and not the economic aspect.

The rules formulated for the Kaliyuga, however, forbid Brahmans to perform sacrifices for the 'lower *varnas*'. The lower *varnas* are enumerated as Washermen, Leather-workers, Dancers, Musicians, Fishermen and Bhilas. Here the expression 'lower *varnas*' is clearly being used to denote certain *jatis*, and from our knowledge of Indian ethnography we know that what these castes have in common (except for the Bhilas) is the polluting nature of their occupations. Thus it is clear that the Brahmans are being forbidden to render ritual services to polluting castes. Here the principle is not that of separation—for the Brahmans are not being simultaneously forbidden from receiving services from them. The general principle is a familiar one, viz. the provision of services to anyone polluted would pollute the giver. This is why only very low Brahmans are found to provide services to polluting castes. On the other hand, receiving from the polluted castes is not only permissible but even necessary, since one of the tasks of the 'polluting' castes is to take away the impurity from the higher castes to whom they provide services. We must stress here that the restriction for the Brahmans is not based on principles of hierarchy, for they are not being forbidden to provide services to all those who are lower than them but only to those who are polluting. Of course, the polluting *jatis* are also the lower ones, but the basis of the restriction is clearly to avoid incurring pollution from the *jatis* enumerated above. Thus the rules regarding exchange of food, women, and services express singly or in combination the three principles of purity-pollution, separation and ranking.

The importance of these principles in understanding commensal relations, marriage, and exchange of services in the caste system has been recognized by most sociologists of caste. Thus each one of the items of exchange has been analysed separately though the exact link among these three items has not been very clearly formulated.

Most sociologists who have written on inter-caste relations have taken food transactions between castes as important clues to an understanding of the ritual position of different castes in the caste hierarchy. However, one finds that while earlier authors such as Srinivas (1952) and Mayer (1960) placed equal importance on the principles of separation, ranking, and purity-pollution in understanding institutionalized commensal relations in the caste system, the recent trend has been to place undue emphasis on hierarchy. Marriott (1968), for instance, has attempted to reconstruct a complete hierarchical ordering of castes in different villages on the basis of food transactions. The basic assumption in Marriott's essay, that the hierarchical ordering of castes is a problem of complete ordering (and not partial ordering) and that food transactions are invariably expressive of ranking, is one instance of how emphasis is shifting from consideration of the principles of separation and purity-pollution to that of ranking in understanding inter-caste relations. It seems to us, however, that unless we place equal emphasis on all three principles, we will not be able to understand the various aspects of the exchange of food, women and services. To take one example, Marriott's contention seems to be that the ban on acceptance of food is always expressive of ranking. However, it has been seen that it is forbidden to accept food from certain categories of people, not because they are 'lower' but because they are 'polluted', and hence have to be 'separated'. Some of the rules in 'Kalidharma-varnana' forbid Brahmans to accept food from those members of their *own jati* who have incurred pollution, and therefore they have to be separated, temporarily or permanently, from the rest. Of course, those who are 'polluted' are those 'who are not of the same status' and hence have to be separated, but clearly the ban on inter-dining in this case does not denote ranking in a hierarchical order. Marriott himself stated later that ' . . . any scoring of Indian competitive actions would remain insufficient if, in Western style, they attended only to the game-like actional outcomes [as in Marriott, 1959 & 1968], and failed to note that the players have at stake also the preservation or transformation of their own natures' (Marriott, 1973). The efforts to understand the system of caste primarily in the context of stratification and ranking misses out this dimension entirely.

Rules regarding the exchange of women as expressive of purity or pollution, separation of *jatis* (through endogamy), or ranking (through hypergamy) have also been extensively studied. The study of hypergamy by Yalman (1971) is particularly useful in understanding the symbolic aspect of the rules of marriage. He clearly sees the link between the exchange of food and exchange of women, but seems to regard this link as a case of some deep-seated psychological identity between food and sex in most cultures. To quote Yalman on this point,

There seems to be a deep psychological identity between eating and sexual intercourse (an identity which is overtly made in diverse cultures) and rules of caste rank utilize both food and sexual intercourse as equally powerful emotionally charged symbols. . . . The relations between castes are always expressed in the complex idiom of food and sex. . . . We must assume that the most universal prohibitions of caste, those of inter-dining and intermarriage, are really different ways of saying the same thing. . . . It should also be underlined that this differentiation between eaters and refusers, women-givers and women-takers lies at the basis of Sinhalese ideas of hypergamy and dowry [Yalman, 1971: 94–5].

The main difficulty in Yalman's analysis seems to be his tendency to equate prohibitions on sexual intercourse with prohibitions on marriage. Having stated that relations between castes are always expressed in the complex idiom of food and sex, he then goes on to conclude that the prohibitions on inter-dining and intermarriage, being based on the symbols of food and sex, are different ways of saying the same thing. While there may be sound reasons for supposing that there is a psychological identity between food and sex, it is clearly unwarranted to equate rules regarding women with whom *sexual* intercourse is permitted with rules regarding women with whom marriage is permitted. In a system of exchange, a woman given in marriage may be regarded as a prestation. On the other hand a woman with whom sexual relations are permitted but not marriage, cannot be similarly regarded. It is at the sociological level that we will have to find an explanation of the identity between food and women; the psychological identity between food and sex does not provide the basis for an explanation.

As has already been indicated, we have found it useful to regard both food and women as prestations, and with the inclusion of ritual services in this universe of discourse, the Dharmaranya Purana leaves us in very little doubt that all three are being regarded as elements of prestations which bring the 'givers' and 'receivers' into some kind of institutionalized relationship. Most of the rules for Kaliyuga are negative and indicate the category of people to whom these prestations cannot be made. Incidentally, we now have the explanation of the rule forbidding Brahmans from accepting food of the house in which a daughter has been given in marriage. Since both 'food' and 'women' are prestations, the 'givers' in the case of one must not become 'receivers' in the case of the other. In other words, the direction of gifts is required to be the same. Here again the difficulties in interpreting the 'receivers of food' and 'the givers of food' as expressive only of ranking are obvious. We cannot conclude from this rule that those who give women are superior to those who receive women simply because the former are forbidden to accept food from the latter. Such an interpretation would contradict our earlier interpretation of the rule that no Brahman may accept money for giving his daughter in marriage. We interpreted this rule to mean that hypogamous marriages are forbidden and therefore whenever there is an asymmetrical exchange of women, the 'receivers of women' are to be placed higher than the 'givers of women'.

In this context, mention must be made of Lévi-Strauss' essay (1963) on 'The Bear and the Barber', which demonstrated the structural transformation between totemism and the caste system, in terms of exchange of food, goods and services, and women. Introducing his approach to the understanding of these two formal institutions, Lévi-Strauss says:

In earlier writings I have tried to show that exchange in human societies is a universal means of ensuring the interlocking of its constitutive parts and that this exchange can operate at different levels, among which the more important are food, goods and services, and women. . . . Sometimes, the three forms (or two of them) are called upon, so to speak, to complement each other either positively or negatively. (p. 4).

The analysis of the *kalidharma* in the Purana is a striking confirmation of the arrangement of these three variables to show the negative relations between *jatis* in the caste system.

To sum up the discussion up to here, the rules regarding the *dharma* to be followed in Kaliyuga define the relationships between *jatis*. These relationships are defined through the use of a set of symbols, viz. food, women, and services. These three are treated as components of prestations and elaborate rules are laid down regarding the exchange of these prestations. We inferred from the textual material describing these rules that the principles which form the bases of these rules are those of separation, ranking, and purity-pollution. It is hoped that the link between the three symbols on the one hand, which has not been explicitly recognized, and between the three principles which form the bases of these rules, on the other, will be sufficiently clear from the preceding section. We shall now proceed to show how the principles of purity-pollution, separation and ranking explain the further divisions within the Trivedi and Chaturvedi groupings respectively.

The Trivedis were divided among the Dhenujas and other Trivedis. The Dhenuja caste was composed of those young boys who had sex-relations with widows and unmarried girls. The boys were married off to these women when it was found that the women had conceived. From the story it is clear that the Dhenujas had broken the rules prescribed for the exchange of women in Kaliyuga. Their relations with the women were illicit in the first instance, since the women were not their wives. However, what was considered important by the Brahmans was the fact that the boys belonged to the wrong *varna* category (see the reference to the *varna-samkara*) and therefore the children born of these unions would belong to the *golaka* and *kanina* categories. The Brahmans were worried that if the children were allowed to be affiliated to their mothers' caste, they would pollute the entire caste. Thus the women and their unborn children who had the potential of polluting the entire Trivedi caste were separated from it to form a separate division. Fission in this instance resulted from the operation of the principles of pollution and separation. Incidentally, this provides some scriptural support to Yalman's (1963) suggestion that hypogamous sexual relations are considered heinous in the caste system because of the problems of affiliation that would arise if the women were to become pregnant by men of lower castes.

Among the Chaturvedis, the three divisions which were separated from the other Chaturvedis were the Mallas, the Tanduliyas and an unnamed division of 111 Chaturvedis. The Mallas were separated for three reasons. First, they took to fighting with their hands. Second, they had promiscuous relations with other men's wives. Finally, they took on customs of foreign lands which made their identity doubtful.

The Tanduliyas had to resort to the mode of livelihood of the Vanikas (*Vanika vritti*) and also took on customs of foreign lands. The 111 Chaturvedis who had refused to accept gifts from Rama had to do the same and therefore they became different from other Chaturvedi Brahmans.

It is clear from the above discussion that Mallas, Tanduliyas, and the 111 Chaturvedis became separate from the other Chaturvedis because of the different kind of services that they rendered. Thus the other Chaturvedis are opposed to these three divisions taken together, for while the former performed sacrifices, the latter did not. Within the three divisions the Mallas were different from the other two since they made their living through fighting with their hands while the other two were engaged in *Vanika vritti*. Finally, the 111 Chaturvedis were distinguished from the Tanduliyas from the manner in which they adopted the occupation of Vanikas, the former having adopted it because they refused to accept the gifts of Rama and the latter because they could not face the hazards of the journey to the forest to please Hanumana. The differences in all the divisions are further buttressed by the 'foreign customs' which the Mallas, Tanduliyas, and the 111 Chaturvedis adopted.

It is of some interest to examine the meaning of an occupation such as wrestling in this context. In the Dharmaranya Purana the Jethimallas are defined as 'defiled' because they gave up their position as officiating priests and took to 'fighting with their hands', i.e. wrestling. It is interesting to see how the Jethimallas themselves interpret the meaning of wrestling in the Malla Purana, which is the Purana specific to this group and was written much later than the Dharmaranya Purana, i.e. in the seventeenth century.[1]

The Malla Purana begins with the establishment of Brahmans in Dharmaranya by King Aama. At this stage the Malla Purana does not distinguish between Mallas and the other Brahmans. It will be recalled that in the Dharmaranya Purana also, the Mallas emerged as a separate division of the Modh Brahmans much later. The Malla Purana, like the Dharmaranya Purana, emphasizes the fact that the Jethimallas who had not emerged as a separate division of the Modh Brahmans in the Treta age had been established in Dharmaranya by King Rama. The King had given them grants and promised them his temporal protection in return for their agreement to officiate in the

---

[1] See Das (1968) for a detailed analysis of this Purana.

fire-sacrifices that Rama wished to offer to his ancestors as well as to the gods.

Where the Malla Purana diverges significantly from the Dharmaranya Purana is in its interpretation of the meaning of wrestling. In the Malla Purana the Brahmans are shown to be engaged in performing fire sacrifices in a hermitage-like atmosphere in a town called Mayuravam Balam (another Sanskritized version of Modhera) in the Treta age. Then in the Dwapara age Krishna and his brother Balabhadra were said to have passed through this town after they had killed Kansa. Krishna was so pleased with the Brahmans that he offered to reveal his highly esoteric *mallavidya* (art of wrestling) to them. The Brahmans, however, were extremely hesitant in accepting this offer for it would involve the acceptance of a new *vritti* (source of livelihood). However, Krishna argued that with the advent of Kaliyuga, which is the age of sin, the kings would not protect the Brahmans. Therefore, he pleaded, it was necessary for the Brahmans to learn the art of wrestling in order that they might protect the *dharma* with its aid. Finally, the Brahmans were convinced by Krishna's argument and they agreed to learn the art of wrestling from Krishna and to use it. Krishna not only taught the Brahmans wrestling but also gave a detailed discourse on various aspects of wrestling including the preparation of the arena for wrestling, a classification of physical exercises, and the rules for arranging wrestling matches. This material can be put to good use for interpreting Hindu notions of space and the concept of the human body. However, these are not of immediate concern to us.

To come back to the symbolic meaning of wrestling, the Malla Purana argues that the mutual dependence between Brahmans and king was likely to be destroyed in the Kaliyuga since kings would not perform their rightful duties. Therefore the Brahmans accepted the art of wrestling as a means of livelihood in order to protect their *dharma*. In this particular context, wrestling is defined as a functional equivalent to the king's protection.

This interpretation of wrestling by the author of the Malla Purana is extremely important in allowing the Mallas claim to Brahmanical status. In the *varna* theory of occupations, each *varna* is ideally associated with one kind of occupation. The Brahmans perform sacrifices, the Kshatriyas are warriors, the Vaishyas are engaged in trade, and the Shudras perform menial services. This simple association of each *varna* with one kind of occupation, however, leaves aside a whole range of occupations which are anomalous, and wrestling would fall in this class of occupations. Clearly it cannot be placed unambiguously under performance of sacrifices, trade, or performance of menial services. By describing wrestling as 'fighting with hands', the Malla Purana implicitly opposes it to 'fighting with weapons', which is the occupation associated with Kshatriyas. Further, fighting with weapons is exogenous, in that it is directed against an enemy while wrestling as practised by Mallas is not directed against anyone as it is for purposes of entertainment. In the last analysis, of course, the Purana contradicts itself, for having defined wrestling as a means for protection of *dharma*, it later goes on to describe it as primarily a means of entertainment.

Coming back to the Dharmaranya Purana, the distinct groups within the Trivedi and Chaturvedi groupings are identified in the myths by the three principles of organization mentioned earlier, viz. descent, locality, and cult-group. Each of the groups in the myth is an endogamous group so that consanguinal relations would stop conceptually at the boundaries of each of these *jatis*. They are further identified by the different localities in which they reside and finally each division has a different deity. Thus in all these cases differences between the different *jatis* are translated into separate diacritical marks based on the principles of descent, locality and cult-group.

VI

Having discussed the conception of fission of castes in the Dharmaranya Purana, we can now go on to discuss the relevance of the results obtained in the previous section. We have already discussed in considerable detail how the conceptual order of Sanskritic Hinduism in terms of the different kinds of relations between the mutually exclusive categories of Brahman, king, and *sanyasi* is relevant to an understanding of the concept of *jati* in the Purana. As we have shown, the myths start at a level of abstraction at which the *jatis* are placed and differentiated from other *jatis* with reference to their place in the conceptual scheme and not with reference to other like units in a linear hierarchical order. The *jatis* are further identified in the myths by a combination of the three principles of organization—descent, locality, and cult-group. The importance of these three principles is evident when one realizes that not only the *jatis*, but also the deities that appear in the text are identified through these three principles, singly or in combination.

In the Dharmaranya Purana we first come across the three deities —Brahma, Vishnu, and Shiva. However, since only Vishnu and Shiva are the objects of cult-groups, the Purana gives a brief myth to account for the absence of any cults woven around Brahma. The story is that once there was a dispute between Vishnu and Brahma as to which of them was greater. They went to Shiva for a resolution of their arguments. He (Shiva) made a *Shiva-linga* expand—the top of the *linga* towards heaven and the bottom towards the nether regions. Then he asked Brahma and Vishnu to go in the direction of heaven and the nether regions respectively. He made a condition that whichever of the two would be the first to return after having worshipped the end of the *linga* on either side, would be regarded as the greater of the two. Brahma mounted his vehicle and started ascending towards heaven but however far he went he could not see the end of the *linga* in sight. On the way he met a *ketaki* (pandanus) flower. Knowing that *ketaki* was the favourite flower of Shiva he induced her to lie to Shiva and say that he (Brahma) had reached the end of the *linga* and worshipped it with *ketaki*. Then both Brahma and *ketaki* returned together and told the fabricated story; Shiva, who knew that they were lying, was enraged. He put a curse on Brahma that he would not be worshipped by anyone on earth and on *ketaki* that she would not be used any longer for the worship of *Shiva-linga*. After a time Vishnu returned from the nether regions and acknowledged his defeat, confessing that he had not been able to reach the end of the *linga*. Shiva was pleased with his truthfulness and blessed him.

In this story we have an apparent justification of the fact that Brahma who figures so prominently in Sanskrit texts is not the centre of any cult-group. On the other hand, references to Vishnu and Shiva in the text take into account their being not only important gods in the Sanskritic pantheon but also centres of important cults. Thus the principle of cult-group is being used here to identify the two deities.

All the other deities that appear in the myths are female. The goddess Shrimata who is described in 'The Sorrows of Shrimata' is the presiding deity of the city, Moheraka, and is clearly the goddess of a locality. The remaining goddesses are identified as either Vaishnavi or Shakti (cult-group affiliation). They are further identified by the different castes to which they belong (descent-group membership). The goddess Paramaranda is born of Vishnu's yawn and is, therefore, a Vaishnavi Devi. She is the caste-goddess of the Trivedis who are exhorted to worship her on all auspicious occasions. The other goddesses (Nimbaja, Chhatra and Bhadrika) are all Shakti in their cult-affiliation and are assigned to the different *jatis* within the Trivedi and Chaturvedi divisions, though the Sanskrit word used for them is *kuladevi*, which means the goddess of lineage. It is obvious that the three principles of social structure, i.e. descent, locality, and cult-group, singly or in combination define the different deities.

The third universe of discourse which we identified in the myths is that of symbolic prestations, comprising food, women, and services. We found that the exchange of these prestations, or rather the restrictions on the exchange, were based on the principles of separation, ranking, and purity/pollution. At this level the description in the Dharmaranya Purana links up with behavioural Hinduism and we find in it all the principles which have been regarded as essential in governing actual relationships between castes. Just as the Purana gives the details regarding the internal differentiation between the Brahmans, so it relates the differentiation among the Vanikas. In a chapter entitled 'Shudra Jati Bheda' the differences among the Modh Vanikas are explained. The story goes as follows.

Once a Gobhuja (name given to the Vanikas when they were created by the three gods, Brahma, Vishnu, and Mahesh) (p. 20) went to the Surya Kunda where he found a *kshapanaka* (Jain mendicant) fast asleep. The mendicant was wearing dirty clothes and was tired and hungry. As the Vanika approached him, the *kshapanaka* quickly got up. The Vanika asked him his name and destination, and since the Jain mendicant looked hungry, he offered to give him food. The Jain mendicant said, 'I was born in a Vanika caste. I have now taken refuge in the Jain *dharma*. I have renounced my wife and my property, and have acquired peace. I do not collect food. I only beg for food which is sufficient for a meal and not more. I do not collect wealth or touch metal. I have pity on all people.' While the mendicant was speaking thus, the Vanika came under his spell and begged him to come to his house for a meal. The Jain mendicant, however, said that he could accept food only from the followers of Jain *dharma* and not from the followers of Vedic *dharma*. At this the Vanika became a disciple of the Jain *dharma*. He took him to his house and asked the other members of his family to accept the ascetic as their spiritual preceptor. Some of the members accepted this while the others denounced the mendicant as a *pakhandi* (a cheat). The Jain mendicant stayed on in the house of this Vanika and soon started giving religious discourses to the other members of the Vanika caste. He would denounce the Vedas and the Brahmans, and all the Vedic gods. Some Vanikas were soon influenced by his denunciations.

After a time, the Trivedi Brahmans learnt about the Jain mendicant. They went to hear him and found him denouncing the Vedas, the gods, and the Brahmans. They were very angry and beat him up. The Brahmans wanted to kill him but at the intervention of some Vanikas refrained from doing so and threw him out of the city. Serious differences of opinion then arose among the Vanikas. Some believed that it was the supreme duty of the Vanikas to serve the Brahmans and they should never have allowed the Jain mendicant to stay amongst them. Therefore they thought that whatever had been done to the mendicant by the Brahmans was justified. Others thought that the behaviour of the Brahmans to the mendicant had been cruel, and so they left with the mendicant for a city called Adalajak. They became a separate Vanika caste and were known as Adalajakas. There were some other Gobhujas who took up the occupation of rowing boats and were called Madhukaras. They lived near the sea. Some worked as Oil-pressers (teli) and were declared outcaste by the other Vanikas.

What seems of interest in the material on 'Shudra Jati Bheda' is the relative simplicity with which the divisions within the Vanika grouping are explained in comparison to the divisions among the Brahmans. Those Vanikas who accepted the Jain faith simply moved away to another town and formed a separate caste. The Dharma-ranya Purana does not seem to see any contradiction in the group which had become converted to Jainism remaining a caste. On the other hand, the conversion of a king was seen as a major threat to the Brahmans and to the Hindu order. This is understandable when we realize that the heretic nature of rebel sects such as the Jain lay in their denial of the categorical partition between Brahman, king, and sanyasi, and not on castes as modes of social grouping. To use an analogy borrowed from linguistics, even when the sects carried the same vocabulary they changed the grammar.

In explaining the varna scheme of relations, it has been often assumed that the four varna categories are homologous categories arranged in an hierarchical order. The hierarchy has not been conceived as linear. Both Dumézil (1958) and Dumont (1970a), for instance, have derived the hierarchy from a series of binary oppositions.

According to this mode of argument the *varna* scheme first posits an opposition between Brahmans and others. Next, it posits sequentially the opposition between Brahmans and Kshatriyas, on the one hand, and the rest of the population, on the other; the twice-born as opposed to the Shudra; and finally the Arya opposed to the Dasyu. The influence of the Dharmasutras on this formulation is obvious. It is, indeed, possible to hold this view as long as we concentrate on the distribution of rights and privileges of the four *varnas*, for in this context the *varnas* are arranged hierarchically, each superior category encompassing the inferior one.

However, when we move away from the distribution of rights and privileges to other themes, we find that it becomes possible to represent the *varna* scheme as a special case of the division of the social into holders of temporal power (king), inherent ritual status (Brahman) and the non-Brahman mass of householders within the caste system. It may be noted that the categories Vanika and Shudra were not lumped together in opposition to Brahmans and Kshatriyas, and then separated in the context of the opposition between twice-born and Shudra, as Dumont's scheme suggests. Instead, the non-Brahman mass of householders were referred to in the text as either Vanikas or Shudras. Similarly, the association between the Kshatriya *varna* and kingship is not absolute. The myths clearly say that the relation between the king and the Brahman does not alter, regardless of whether the king is a Kshatriya or Shudra. Therefore it is clear that the four *varna* categories are not homologous entities.[1] The myths take the Brahman category from the *varna* scheme and the category of *sanyasi* from the *ashrama* scheme. The addition of the category 'kingship' completes the conceptual scheme of Hinduism.

The above formulation may help to explain why the only *varna* category which occurs at both the *varna* and the *jati* level is the category 'Brahman'. The corresponding *jati* category of the Kshatriya *varna* is 'Rajput' (lit. the son or descendant of kings). The Vaishya *varna* has Vanika and Baniya as its corresponding *jati* categories. Interestingly enough, the word Vaishya does not occur often in this version of the Dharmaranya Purana, though the word Vanika occurs frequently. As is well known, the *jatis* corresponding to the Shudra category are indeed numerous and show a wide range of differentiation. This dimension of the problem makes it possible to suggest that

---

[1] From a different point of view, Romila Thapar (1975) has also argued against treating *varna* categories as caste categories.

the sociologists who have seen the consistent failure of rebel sects to break the caste system, in that the sects themselves develop divisions similar to castes, have perhaps missed the essence of the heterodoxy of these sects. In attacking the position of Brahmans the sects were not attacking the caste system but the special position of Brahmans as holders of *inherent* ritual merit within the conceptual scheme of Hinduism. It is no accident that even today while people do not see any contradiction in speaking of groups such as Jain Baniyas, Sikh Khatris, and Muslim Rajputs, they do not conceive of the possibility of Jain Brahmans or Sikh Brahmans or Muslim Brahmans. The chapter on 'Shudra Jati Bheda', in its very poverty of mythologizing, has the merit of showing us that the attack on Brahmans by the rebel sects was not equivalent to an attack on caste as a mode of social grouping. It may be recalled that Modh Brahmans had established a code of conduct which was special to the Kaliyuga. One may question why the text needs the theory of *kalivarjya* to explain actual relationships between castes. It has been rightly pointed out by Pocock (1964) that the theory of *kalivarjya* provides justification for practices which are sanctioned by caste-custom but have no support in the Dharmashastras. However, I believe we can go further and ask the question, 'what is the structural meaning of Kaliyuga in this whole scheme of analysis?'

In trying to understand the meaning of the *yugas* in the Dharmaranya Purana, it will be useful to distinguish between continuous time and discrete time. It is recognized almost universally that (as continuous time) the movement of the four ages in Hindu thought is cyclical. The four ages successively replace each other and the end of the cycle is marked by Kaliyuga being replaced by the Kritayuga. To this we may add that movement of time is symbolized in the text by increasing differentiation of objects, space, people, and deities. In the beginning there is only undifferentiated water and then the physical order is created through differentiation of physical objects. The social order emerges by first being differentiated from the physical order through the creation of Brahmans. Then within the social order, places, people, and deities are differentiated. Thus, in the beginning there are only Brahmans. Then, Brahmans are differentiated from Vanika/Shudras and further progress of time is marked by differentiation within the Brahman category. This differentiation in people is associated with differentiation in places—for each successively differentiated *jati* is associated with a separate locality. Finally, the principles of social structure which are used to differentiate between *jatis* are also used to differentiate between deities and gradually there is an emergence of separate deities of localities, descent groups and cult-groups. Thus the succession of *yugas* is symbolized by this increasing differentiation in the various spheres. Finally, in the typical Puranic style when the end of Kaliyuga comes, all beings are destroyed and only the undifferentiated water is left. The course of creation begins again. Thus time moves in a continuous pendular movement between undifferentiated mass to differentiated order.

Besides this underlying conception of time as a continuous pendular movement, there is a parallel conception of *yugas* in terms of discrete time, where the first *yuga*, the Krita age, is opposed to the Kaliyuga in terms of their character. This is why practices which were allowed in the first age are not allowed in the Kaliyuga. In a brief paper called 'Time and Dharma', Lingat (1962) examines the problem of how the Hindu theory of '*ekavakyatva*', or the theory that rules of *dharma* are expressions of an eternal law derived from the Vedas, is reconciled with the theory of *kalivarjya*. He quotes from various sources in Sanskrit to show that the *validity* of the rules of *dharma* is not lost in the Kaliyuga. In fact rules of conduct which were upheld in the Kritayuga continue to remain so in the Kaliyuga. It is only man's own growing weakness and loss of moral sense that prevents him from deriving spiritual benefit from these rules and thus causes them to be prohibited. Thus in terms of discrete time, the Kritayuga is structurally opposed to the Kaliyuga. Now since we know that Hindus have always lived in the Kaliyuga, the problem is why this structural opposition had to be posited in Hindu thought. Addressing himself to a similar problem, Pocock (1964) has tried to analyse the meaning of Kaliyuga and has come to the significant conclusion that Kaliyuga is not *homologous* to the other *yugas* but is *opposed* to them. This move from a 'sociology of harmonious relations' to a 'sociology of contradictions' helps to restate the problem but does not provide a solution. The crux of our problem is that for an anthropologist, not only is a people's factual past important but also the *conception* of their past, for the latter is a part of a people's structural present. It is in this sense that we have to explore the meaning of the opposition between the Kritayuga and the Kaliyuga.

In the Dharmaranya Purana we find that the myths which relate to the conceptual order of Hinduism were relegated to the past. The creation of Brahmans and Vanikas took place in the Kritayuga and the myths establishing their opposition relate to the first age. In the Tretayuga, the principle of temporal power was introduced through Rama and the myths relating to this age established the relation of exchange between Brahman and king. The events in the reign of King Aama are said to have taken place in the third age, the Dwaparyuga. In this *yuga* the heretic sects were introduced which disturbed the structural order of Hinduism, though this structure was finally reinstated through the efforts of the Trivedi Brahmans. Finally, it is only in the Kaliyuga that the Purana establishes a new code of behaviour which finds no sanction in the Dharmashastras or in myths relating to the earlier *yugas*. Thus it seems quite clear that while the earlier *yugas* stand for the conceptual order necessary to Hinduism, the rules relating to Kaliyuga stand for the principles which govern actual relationships between castes.

If we look at the whole problem from the point of view of the Modh Brahmans we can see that their caste Purana starts by placing them in the conceptual order of Hinduism. This is done for a series of segmentary units. Thus they are placed in the conceptual order first as Brahmans versus others, then as Modh Brahmans versus other Brahmans, then as Trivedis versus Chaturvedis and finally as Dhenujas versus other Trivedis, and Mallas, Tanduliyas and 111 Chaturvedis versus other Chaturvedis. Having placed each of these divisions—from the largest to the smallest—in the conceptual order of Hinduism, the Purana then goes on to define their actual relationships with other empirical groups. The code governing these relationships is formulated for the Kaliyuga. The relation between the other *yugas* and Kaliyuga, then, is that of the conceptual order to the empirical order. This seems to be the reason why the Purana of a particular caste has to begin with the creation of the world and then has to come down to the caste, its divisions and relationships with other castes. This is because the latter can be discussed only after the caste has been placed in the conceptual order of Hinduism which, as just shown, is relegated to the earlier *yugas*, so that the Purana has to begin with the Kritayuga even if it is primarily concerned with a *jati* like the Modh Brahmans.

VII

A complete explanation of the structure of Dharmaranya Purana has now been given. The attempt has been to work out the postulates of

Sanskritic Hinduism through this Purana, very similar to the linguistics specialist's attempt to decode an unknown language. In the process of our analysis we have tried to show the three different levels of abstraction in the Purana. It is important to remember that the level of abstraction has to be specified when talking of the principles of Hinduism. For instance, while hierarchy does not figure as a principle of organization at the level of defining the conceptual order of Hinduism or at the level of the principles which serve to identify empirical groups, it is of importance in understanding the rules which govern actual relationships between castes. Similarly, the meaning of certain words in the text is understandable only when the context is clearly specified.

To take an example: In the earlier part of the Purana, the word Shudra is used interchangeably with the word Vanika, and clearly these two words stand for the non-Brahman mass of householders within the caste system. However, in the chapter 'Kalidharma-varnana' we frequently come across the expression, 'to be avoided like a Shudra'. In this context, the word Shudra comes to stand for someone who is polluting and hence has to be avoided. Thus the meaning of the word Shudra changes in accordance with whether the reference is to the conceptual order of Hinduism or to the empirical order. It is for this reason necessary to carry out detailed analyses of the Sanskrit texts pertaining to different periods in order to understand the meaning of concepts like *varna* and *ashrama*, and not to begin by assuming that the meaning of these concepts is clearly understood.

4

Concepts of Space*

I

IN THE last decade there has been a marked interest in the analysis of native systems of classification and in the symbolism of laterality. In the Indian context, it is being realized that the opposition between right and left is not a peripheral distinction but is of central importance in understanding different aspects of Hindu social categorization. Thus the distinction between right and left is used for classifying castes and sects and is also fundamental in partitioning the human body for purposes of ritual. Our analysis of the Grihya Sutra of Gobhila shows that the opposition between the antithetical concepts of right and left and the four cardinal points provide fundamental categories for the symbolization of ideas like fertility, prosperity, life and death.

As has been mentioned in the Introduction, the Grihya Sutras were largely compiled on the basis of observed domestic rituals and it may be for this reason that while the *shrauta* rituals have practically disappeared, there are recognizable similarities between the domestic rituals described in the Grihya Sutras and those practised by devout Hindus even today. While observing domestic rites among the Hindus one is frequently impressed by the importance attached to the right/left opposition. For instance, there are clearly formulated rules about the contexts in which either the right or the left hand is to be used. Similarly, the direction of movement in these rituals is clearly specified. For example, the contexts in which an object has to be circumambulated by placing it to one's left are differentiated from those in which it is to be placed to one's right. Again, meticulous care

*This chapter appeared in a slightly different form in *Text and Context: The Social Anthropology of Tradition*, edited by Ravindra K. Jain. Copyright © 1977 by ISHI, Institute for the Study of Human Issues, Philadelphia; reproduced by permission of the Institute.

is taken about the direction which the subject of a rite faces. Manuals of rituals, such as the ones brought out by sectarian organizations like the Arya Samaj for the correct performance of *yajnas* (fire-sacrifices), also contain clear and detailed instructions on these matters.

Yet field observations of Hindu rituals rarely describe the exact rules that are observed on these occasions. This may be either because the rules are not considered important by the informants, or the field-worker is not sensitive to the variations in them and has therefore failed to question his informants on these matters. Moreover, while describing various ritual acts, anthropologists very often resort to descriptive categories which do not have any counterpart in native languages. For instance, Srinivas (1952:117) uses terms like 'clockwise' and 'anti-clockwise movements' in his study of the Coorg ritual though there are no native terms corresponding to clockwise and anti-clockwise movement. Srinivas's *description* may not be any less clear for his using non-native categories but this is probably an impediment to his analysis and masks the code behind the formalized system of ritual and belief.

II

This section analyses the dichotomous division between right and left and the general categorization of space in the ritual procedures described in the Grihya Sutra of Gobhila. Its immediate concern is not the relation between the rules framed in the texts and their observance in practice. Obviously there will be many variations according to region, caste and sect in the performance of domestic ceremonies. However, the rules about spatial categories are likely to exhibit greater uniformities than other rules. This is because spatial categories, at the surface, seem to be more neutral and subject to less manipulation. It may not be accidental that while many other rules relating to domestic ceremonies have been questioned by reformers or by members of rebel sects, we are not aware of a single sect which has tried to question the rules regarding the use of right and left, or south and east. Secondly, it should be noted that following the general approach here, unless the meanings attached to spatial categories are discussed through an analysis of one particular system it will not be possible to understand the variations. Since problems of tractability are more easily resolved by adopting a monographic framework of analysis, a single text has been chosen for the analysis.

The purpose, of course, is to understand as a symbolic system the domestic ceremonies described in this manual of ritual.

Description of Domestic Ceremonies

The Grihya Sutras deal with different types of domestic ceremonies. These ceremonies centre around the sacred fire that every house-holder is expected to establish on setting up his house. There are four types of ceremonies described in the Grihya Sutra of Gobhila, and there is in addition a miscellaneous universe of discourse. The principles of classification which the text uses to describe the various types of domestic ceremonies will become clear as the analysis proceeds.

The first type of ceremonies relates to the rituals which are to be performed when the domestic fire is first established. The usual prescription for this in the Grihya Sutras is that the sacred fire should be set up either at the end of the period of study or at the time of marriage. Gobhila begins with the setting up of the fire at the conclusion of the period of study. The second type of ritual acts relates to fire sacrifice which a householder should perform at various fixed points of time, e.g. daily fire sacrifices to be performed in the morning and evening, fortnightly fire sacrifices to be performed at the advent of the new-moon and full-moon, and fire sacrifices to be performed at the time of harvesting. In addition there are some prescribed sacrifices to be performed in the 'dark' months of winter for protection from snakes. But for reasons which will become clear later these sacrifices are described along with regular yearly fire-sacrifices to ancestors. The third type of ceremonies are those which have to be performed at various rites of transition, e.g. marriage, pregnancy, childbirth, tonsure, initiation, etc.

Rites to be performed for ancestors in the months of winter every year are of a fourth type. These rites are described as separate from rites to be performed on occasions of marriage, childbirth, etc. The rites for ancestors are described along with ceremonies to be performed for protection from snakes and, as we shall show later, there is a structural identity between the two. Textbooks on the history of Sanskrit literature often mention that the 'burial of the dead' (*sic*) is an important theme in the Grihya Sutras (cf. Macdonell, 1899; Oldenberg, 1892). In fact, the rites at cremation are often thought to belong to the same class as the rites to ancestors. However, it may be pointed out here that the only Grihya Sutra which describes the procedure to be followed at cremation is that of Ashvalayana. The other Grihya Sutras, such as those of Gobhila, Hiranyakeshina, and Apastamba do not deal with this subject at all. In contrast to this, descriptions of other rites such as marriage, propitiation of ancestors, full-moon and new-moon sacrifices are found in all the Grihya Sutras. Therefore it seems likely that cremation of the dead was not an intrinsic part of the *grihya* (domestic) rituals. This contention is supported by an examination of the nature of the Ashvalayana Grihya Sutra. Indologists are agreed that the author of the Ashvalayana Shrauta Sutra himself wrote the Ashvalayana Grihya Sutra and considered the latter to be a continuation of the former.

The part in which the rites to be followed for the cremation of a dead body are described begins with the general description, 'If one who has lit the Shrauta fires dies . . . ' The number of fires to be lit for the cremation are three—a number which characterizes the *shrauta* fires and not the *grihya* fire. Further, in the rites for ancestors, which are performed in specially dug pits for fathers, the sacrificer is given the option of either lighting the fire in the pits from the *shrauta* fires which are already alight, or if he has not lighted the *shrauta* fires then he should take the flame from his eternally burning *grihya* fire. In the former case, three fires must be lighted and in the latter case only one fire is lighted. In view of this, it seems significant that the *grihya* fire is not used for lighting the cremation fires. One would probably be justified in concluding that death is not seen as an event primarily concerning the domestic group in a way in which marriage is. The Hindu ideal that a person should die outside his house near some source of holy waters has already been discussed in the Introduction. The Ashvalayana Grihya Sutra also advises a person who falls ill to leave his village and go elsewhere. If he recovers, he should return and perform a thanksgiving sacrifice. If he dies, his dead body should be cremated at a suitable place. From the internal evidence of the texts, as well as the structure of ideas, it seems erroneous to consider the cremation rites and rites to ancestors as belonging to a single class.

In addition to the rites described above, the text also suggests a set of rites for the fulfilment of specific wishes—such as those for discovering hidden treasure, attaining fame, etc. These are clearly not obligatory on the householder.

The Right/Left Opposition

In the case of all the rituals mentioned above, the text lays great emphasis on a clear specification of the use of the right and left sides. In fact the right/left opposition is so important that it runs through the entire text. This is, of course, not a surprising finding. The different characteristics of the right and the left hand, and their importance in different cultures, was recognized by Hertz (1960) as early as 1909. He had argued that the right and left sides can be shown to be associated in a consistent manner with the sacred and the profane (in the sense of negatively sacred) respectively in a large number of cultures.[1] Thus the right hand, according to him, is the hand which is used for worship and for the performance of various pure tasks. The impure tasks, according to him, are usually relegated to the left hand which is also considered to be particularly adept in dealing with demons, magical practices and sorcery. In the Indian context, however, the attention given to the opposition of pure and impure has been so overwhelming that the right/left opposition has been subsumed under this general opposition of pure and impure.

An attempt will be made to show that such an identification of right with pure and left with impure is not correct. In Hindu ritual there are clearly specified contexts in which the left hand is used for offering worship, as for instance, to ancestors which if it were primarily an impure hand it would not be eligible for. An attempt will also be made to show that none of the oppositions which Hertz associated with the right/left opposition such as that of religion and magic, gods and demons, priest and shaman, are sufficient to explain the complexity of the right/left opposition in Hindu ritual. In order to explore the various meanings associated with the right and the left let us examine the different contexts in which the use of the right or the left is prescribed in this Grihya Sutra.

Three different types of rules have been formulated about the use of the right or the left in the Grihya Sutra. There are some contexts in which the use of the one side is prescribed and the other proscribed. For instance, oblations to the fire during the wedding ceremony have to be given with the right hand while the oblations to ancestors during the periodic ancestor-worship have to be given with the left hand. Secondly, we find a number of contexts in which the direction

[1] There is a departure in Hertz's usage of the term profane from Durkheim's. As is well known, the term profane was closer to the category 'mundane' in Durkheim who did not consider sacred to be equivalent to good.

of movement is prescribed either from right to left or from left to right. For instance, in the fortnightly rituals performed at the domestic fire to mark the advent of the new-moon and full-moon the sacrificial food has to be stirred, while cooking, from left to right. In the rituals to ancestors, or in the rituals to be performed for protection from snakes, the food has to be stirred from right to left. Thirdly, there are contexts in which both the right and left are used but precedence is given to one over the other. For instance, in the tonsure ceremony, both the right and left sides of the child's head have to be shaved but the right side has to be shaved first. Similarly, while pounding grain during the new-moon and full-moon ceremonies the right hand is placed above the left, but in the ancestor-propitiation ceremonies the same action has to be performed by placing the left hand above the right.

Now let us see the different contexts in which the texts give explicit prescriptions for the use of right and left.

Right

1. The sacrificial cord which a householder wears must be suspended over the left shoulder so that it hangs from left to right when performing fire-sacrifices relating to (a) daily oblations to be offered on the domestic fire in the morning and the evening, (b) in rites performed at full-moon and new-moon, (c) in rites associated with marriage, pregnancy, childbirth, tonsure, initiation, etc. and (d) in rites performed at the harvest and first-fruit festivals. When a person is wearing his sacrificial cord in this manner he is known as *yajnopavitin*.

2. During the setting up of the domestic fire for the first time and during the marriage ceremony, the subject of the ritual has to circumambulate the fire so that his right side is towards the fire.

3. In rituals associated with morning and evening oblations, full-moon and new-moon ceremonies, marriage, pregnancy, childbirth, tonsure, name-giving and initiation, the right side should be used to the exclusion of the left. For instance, the groom and the bride must offer oblations to the fire with their right hands. Similarly, during some rites in the ceremony the groom must touch the right shoulder of the bride with his right hand. To give another instance, as soon as the child is born the father should smear its tongue with barley and pounded rice using the thumb and fourth finger of his right hand.

4. In all the rituals mentioned above the movement of objects or

persons is always from left to right. The sacrificial food cooked for these occasions has to be stirred from left to right. In rituals to be performed for the new-born babe or in the name-giving ceremony the child must always be passed from the left side to the right side. Similarly, in rituals to be performed at the end of the period of study under a guru the student always moves from left to right.

5. In all these rituals when both hands have to be used, as for the ritual pounding of paddy, the right hand is placed above the left hand.

6. Though in oblations offered to ancestors, whether in the course of daily fire-sacrifice or in the periods prescribed for such purposes during the year, the left predominates over the right, there are a few places in these ceremonies in which the use of the right is prescribed. For instance, there are three pits which are dug for ancestors in a special enclosure during the annual propitiation ceremony. In the middle pit, oblations[1] are made with the formula, 'Adoration to you, O fathers, for the sake of terror, for the sake of sap' and this oblation has to be offered by turning the palm of the left hand upwards. But in the other two oblations which are made at the first and the third pit, the formulae say 'Adoration to you, O fathers, for the sake of life and vital breath' and 'Adoration to you, O fathers, for the sake of comfort'. These two oblations have to be made with the palm of the right hand turned upwards.

Left

1. In the rites performed for ancestors and for protection from serpents, the subject has to wear his sacrificial cord suspended from the right shoulder towards the left side of the abdomen. When the sacrificial cord is worn in this position the subject is known as *prachinavitin*.

2. The direction of all movements, when the rite is connected with ancestors or snakes, is from right to left. For instance, the ritual implements for these occasions have to be fetched from right to left. While cooking the sacrificial food, the pot ladle has to be stirred from right to left.

3. Liquid oblations to serpents, ancestors, and a few other deities whom we shall mention later have to be poured from right to left.

[1] These are not oblations to the fire. They may be oblations of food, a piece of linen, etc. As already explained, the sacrificer may either light three fires or one, depending on whether the fire is taken from the *shrauta* fires or the *grihya* fire.

When the annual ancestor-propitiation ceremony is being held the left side predominates over the right in the entire ritual. However, even on other occasions such as daily fire-sacrifices, harvest and first-fruit sacrifices, and sacrifices to be performed on the fulfilment of specific wishes, some oblations have to be made to ancestors. On these occasions, though the right predominates over the left generally, the oblations to ancestors have to be poured from the right to the left.

4. Oblations to serpents and ancestors have to be made with the left hand.

5. As mentioned earlier, in the course of the annual propitiation of ancestors, when oblations are made with the formula, 'Adoration to you, O fathers, for the sake of terror, for the sake of sap', the palm of the left hand has to be turned upwards.

6. When both hands have to be used in any rite connected with ancestors or serpents, the left hand should be placed above the right hand.

7. In the course of some rituals, there is a specific rite for driving away demons, 'dispellers of wealth' and other undesirable elements. This is done by throwing a blade of holy grass (durva) towards the left, using the left hand for the purpose. The ritual formula accompanying this rite is 'The demons, the dispellers of wealth, have been driven away'.

8. One particular context in the use of the left hand which seems exceptional and must, therefore, be mentioned here relates to the tonsure ceremony. As mentioned earlier, the right side dominates over the left in the ritual. However, when the child's head is first symbolically shaven with a ritual razor made of wood, a person touches the child's head with the holy durva grass, first on the right side, then the back and then the left side, using his left hand for the purpose.

This description shows that the right side has precedence over the left in rituals to mark the passage of time, as in the morning and evening oblations to the domestic fire and the fortnightly oblations to be offered to the fire on the advent of the new-moon and full-moon. Similarly, in all rites of transition except death the use of the right side is prescribed. In contrast, in all rites to ancestors as also in rites for protection from snakes, the use of the left side is prescribed. In the rituals in which the right side dominates, oblations are always made to deities that are conceived as basically benevolent and kind.

In the other rituals, the ancestors provide the main focus and when oblations are made to deities in the course of ancestor-propitiation ceremonies, these are usually deities who inspire terror and are explicitly associated with death, such as Rudra.

The opposition between right and left, thus, is clearly associated with 'rites to gods' and 'rites to ancestors'—the former being associated with propitiation of divine beings who are friendly and benevolent, the latter being associated with those supernatural beings who have to be appeased, who inspire terror and have the potential of causing great harm if they are not regularly propitiated. The opposition between the pairs, right/left and gods/ancestors, is further associated with a number of antithetical pairs, such as even/odd, day/night, vegetables/meat and sundry others.

In view of the importance attached to the pure and impure in Indian sociology the readers' attention should be explicitly drawn to the fact that the opposition between pure and impure is not attached in the text to any of the antithetical pairs in the series that have been mentioned above. In the rites in which the right side dominates, the sacrificial offerings consist of vegetables and grain, the number of Brahmans to be invited is even, and the sacrificial food which is left over is consumed by the householder and his family. In the rites to ancestors and serpents, in which the left side dominates, the sacrificial food consists of grain and meat, the number of Brahmans to be invited is odd (three being the number most often prescribed) and the sacrificial food which is offered to ancestors cannot be (with one exception to be mentioned later) consumed by the householder and his family. Instead, it must be burnt in the fire, thrown in the water, or given away to Brahmans. The rites to gods are said to be dear to the day and the sun, while rites to ancestors and serpents are rites of darkness, dear to the night and have to be performed in the winter months, the 'dark half of the year'.

In fact the text stresses the opposition between the two types of rituals so emphatically that the technical terms used for the sacrifice, the sacrificial food and even the *durva* grass which is strewn on each of these occasions, are different. When offering oblations to ancestors, the sacrificer is known as '*yajnopavitin*', symbolized by his sacrificial cord hanging from the left shoulder towards the right side. When he is offering oblations to ancestors his cord is suspended from the right shoulder to the left side and he is known as '*prachinavitin*'. The holy *durva* grass which is strewn around the domestic fire during these two rites is also of different types. The grass strewn for rites to gods is 'cut from the place where the blades diverge from the stalk' while the grass strewn for rites to ancestors is cut from the root. The sacrificial food offered to the gods is known as *agya* while the sacrificial food offered to ancestors is known as '*pinda*'[1] or '*bali*'. This series of anti-thetical pairs, taken together, express an opposition between the two sides of the ultramundane, one relating to the good and benevolent, and the other relating to appeasement of beings that can cause terror and discomfort. Nothing expresses it more beautifully than rites performed during ancestor-propitiation when the palm of the right hand is held up when oblations are offered to ancestors for the sake of 'life, vital breath and comfort' but the palm of the left hand is held up when the oblation is made 'for the sake of terror, for the sake of sap'.

Despite the fact that a number of observers have been so impressed by the uniqueness of Hindu religious beliefs (e.g. Dumont, 1970), one finds that the opposition of the right and left, the association of the former with life, vital breath and comfort, and the latter with terror and sap, is not unique to Hindus.

In his essay on the right hand, Hertz drew attention to the fact that the right side is often the side of the sacred and the left that of the profane and impure. He wrote:

It is a notion current among the Maori that the right is the 'side of life' (and of strength) while the left is the 'side of death' (and of weakness). Fortunate and life-giving influences enter us from the right and through our right side; and, inversely, death and misery penetrate to the core of our being from the left. . . . In worship man seeks above all to communicate with sacred powers, in order to maintain and increase them, and to draw to himself the benefits of their action. Only the right hand is fit for these beneficial relations, since it participates in the nature of the things and beings on which the rites are to act. The gods are on our right. . . . But worship does not consist entirely in the trusting adoration of friendly gods. Man would willingly forget the sinister powers which swarm at his left, but he cannot; . . . A considerable part of a religious cult, and not the least important part, is devoted to containing or appeasing spiteful or angry supernatural beings, to banishing or destroying bad influences. In this domain it is the left hand that prevails: it is directly concerned with all that is demoniacal. [Hertz, 1960: 101–5].

---

[1] It seems that priests specializing in death rituals interpret '*pinda dana*' offered to the ancestors as a symbolic recreation of the body, which is then gifted to the ancestor (Kaushik, 1976).

Hertz is correct in stating that left is associated with death and demoniacal beings. But surely death is associated with not only demons but also ancestors, with both the *preta* (ghosts) and the *pitri* (fathers). Ancestors come to share the powers which the demons possess but they also have a direct interest in the continuation of their lines and hence the welfare of their descendants. It is notable that in the formulae accompanying the fire-sacrifices in which, the right side dominates and the benevolent deities are worshipped, the dominant theme is that of subjugation to the gods. In the hymns accompanying the rites to ancestors the major theme is the reciprocity between the householder and his ancestors.

During the performance of the ancestor-propitiation ceremony for instance, the householder looks at his own house and addressing his ancestors says, 'Give us a house, O fathers'. Then he looks at the *pinda* offering that he has made, saying 'May we give you an abode, O fathers'. The same is repeated for food, clothes, etc. and special formulae are recited so that the householder may beget good progeny. One of the verses with which the ancestor-propitiation ends is, 'Go away, O fathers, friends of *soma*, on your hidden, ancient paths. After a month return again to our house which will be rich in offspring, in valiant sons, and consume our offerings.'

Thus, though ancestors have the power to cause great harm, they also have the potential and the interest to bestow wealth and progeny on their descendants. Unlike the demons, then, they do not have to be driven away or simply appeased but they have to be propitiated so that they may grant these boons to their descendants. The association between ancestors, material prosperity and progeny is symbolized in the rituals in a number of ways. In the course of the fire-sacrifice performed in the mornings and the evenings some offerings are made to ancestors. Significantly, one of these offerings has to be placed on the bed of the householder, 'so that Kama, the god of love, is pleased'. One does not need very much imagination to see that ancestors are conceptualized as the appropriate persons to bless the procreative activities of the householder. Similarly another offering is made at the entrance of the house so that 'riches may enter'.

It is stated in the Grihya Sutra that during the ancestor-propitiation rituals the *pinda* offered to the grandfather of the householder should be eaten by his (householder's) wife if she is desirous of a son. This association is not surprising since ancestors are themselves dependent upon the continuation of the line of descent. But in addition, we

8

contend that what is being postulated here is a basic non-duality between the person who is offering the sacrifice and the person to whom the sacrifice is being offered. The ancestor is himself, through a cycle of rebirth, the descendant. Thus the meaning of gift and sacrifice itself to ancestors and other deities associated with them is opposite in meaning to the sacrifice offered to the deities in which the right side dominates. In the latter case, the duality of the deity and the sacrifices is emphasized, hence the theme of subjugation dominates. In the former case the paradigm type is the sacrifice of Purusha 'of himself to himself, aided by the gods', hence the dominant theme of reciprocity emerges here.

It must be pointed out, however, that the ancestors are not conceived as benevolent beings as in the case of China. They are clearly threatening beings who are to be feared but whose great potential can be harnessed for the welfare of the householder and his descendants. This combination of awesome and terror-striking characteristics along with the capacity to be easily pleased is also found in other deities of the Hindus. Rudra, for instance, who is the god of death and destruction, is also the lord of demons (Bhutanath) and the one who is most easily pleased (Bholanath) by his devotees. The deities who combine these aspects are usually deities of the left and have been the central sacred figures round which the left hand sects (the *vampanthis*) and the Tantric sects have been built.

The association of the deities of the left with death, night, magical powers, and terror is not confined to the Grihya Sutras. In the study of Konku society, Beck (1972) relates a number of folk myths which show a similar association. Beck has argued that the right/left division is an important principle behind the organization of caste in South India. She finds that the deities of the left hand castes are usually female and are associated with death, sorcery, serpents, and darkness. They usually recruit followers by resorting to various tricks and succeed in establishing themselves as clan or lineage goddesses. Reproduced below is one of the stories associated with Anka Lamman, the clan goddess of some high-ranking left-hand castes in Konku.

Anka Lamman continued her wanderings for many years. However, one day she decided it was time to have a proper temple constructed where her devotees could worship her. The thought of a very wealthy Acari came to her mind. She knew that he had both the means and the skills appropriate for the task. He was a very powerful government official, a *Tahsildar*, or top-ranking administrator at the Taluk level, and she knew that he was afraid of no one. He was so wealthy that he had a palace surrounded by eight walls, but he also had the sorrow of having only one son. Anka Lamman decided to persuade him to build her temple and asked her priest to go to him to make the request.

The priest filled a special ceremonial pot with ash from the burning ground as a sign of his goddess and set off. When he reached the palace he asked to see the Acari, but the latter refused to be summoned by anyone. So the priest had to make his way through seven gates, past seven grounds, in order to confront the man in person. When the priest told the Acari that Anka Lamman had asked that he build her a temple the man became angry. He told his assistants to tie up the priest and beat him. The priest pleaded for mercy with his punishers, however, and was released after a light beating. As the priest ran away, the wealthy Acari shouted after him that he would not build a temple for a goddess of the burning ground. He told the priest he should instead pull out Anka Lamman's teeth—a common remedy for suspected sorcery—and beat her to death.

The priest told all this to the goddess but she responded by asking him to return to the Acari's house. She promised him some special *mantras* ('magical verses') which she told him to place in various spots around the palace. The priest did this. Then Anka Lamman caused the house to fall into darkness in the middle of the day. She also gave the Acari's only son a severe stomach-ache. The Acari quickly sent a servant to fetch a light from the window ledge, but this woman was bitten by a scorpion. Then a second girl, sent to get firewood, was bitten by a snake. Finally, the Acari began to suspect.that all these misfortunes might be due to the goddess Anka Lamman, whose teeth he had earlier said should be pulled. At that very moment an old woman, who was the goddess Anka Lamman in disguise, made her way to the house, and, in telling the Acari's fortune, confirmed his interpretation of events. He then asked this woman if the stomach-ache, the scorpion sting, and the snake-bite would be cured if he agreed to accept Anka Lamman as his *kula teyyam*, or clan goddess and build a temple for her. Anka Lamman agreed to this bargain, but threatened to visit the Acari with further difficulties if he did not carry through with the promise of the temple, and in addition if he did not name all his succeeding children after her. [Beck, 1972: 97–100].

The association of Anka Lamman with the burning ground (signifying death), sorcery, serpents, snakes, and darkness is striking. It is also interesting to note that Anka Lamman establishes herself as a *clan* goddess and hence has the status of an ancestress. She bestows more children on her devotee but makes the condition that he name his children after her. Thus the themes which we found to be associated with ancestors in the worship of whom the left side dominates, are found to be repeated in the case of mythology associated with the left-hand deities of the Konku region. Similarly, folk-mythology of the left-hand sects can be shown to have themes which are variants of this structural pattern. We shall discuss the importance of this in the concluding section.

The Cardinal Points

We shall now take up the meaning of the four cardinal points in the domestic ceremonies described in the Grihya Sutra of Gobhila. In order to avoid unnecessary repetition, we shall not enumerate all the contexts in which the cardinal points are categorized, but the major contexts are given below:

East

1. In the preparation of all rites to gods (e.g. new-moon and full-moon rituals, marriage, pregnancy, etc.) the sacred site is prepared by drawing lines on the ground, as shown in the following diagram. Three of these lines are drawn from west to east.

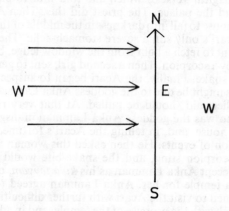

2. Before commencing the fire-sacrifice the householder is directed to strew the ground with the sacred *durva* grass. The direction in which the blades of grass should point vary according to the type of ritual being performed. In the case of the morning and evening oblations, and also for the new-moon and full-moon ceremonies, the blades of grass should point towards the east.

3. The sacred fire is placed to the east of the house for the rituals of marriage, pregnancy, rituals of childhood and initiation.

4. In the case of rituals of marriage and pregnancy, the subject

(bride or pregnant woman) is required to sit on the western side of the fire but she must face the east.

5. At the conclusion of the ritual to mark the end of a person's period of study, the subject drives away either in the eastern or northern direction.

6. When a cow has to be sacrificed, its head should be towards the east and feet towards the north if the rite is sacred to the gods. However, care must be taken to see that no blood is spilt towards the east.

7. If one is desirous of fame one should build a house with its door towards the east.

North

1. While preparing the sacred site, one line has to be drawn from the south to the north.

2. The sacrificial food on the occasion of the new-moon and full-moon ceremonies has to be placed on northward pointing grass.

3. During the rituals of marriage, pregnancy, childhood, and initiation, the subject is required to sit on northward pointing grass.

4. During the performance of these rituals, various ritual movements have to be made from south to north. For instance, during the birth ritual the mother passes the child to the father from south to north. Similarly in the marriage ritual when all the oblations have been made the husband stands towards the southern side of the bride and faces the northern side for the rite of holding his bride's hands and reciting some *mantras*.

West

1. The respective subjects in the rituals of marriage, pregnancy, childbirth and other childhood rituals sit on the western side of the fire on northward pointing grass. The subjects themselves should be facing the east.

2. For the performance of the rites to ancestors a special enclosure has to be built on the southern side of the house. The entrance to this enclosure has to be towards the west.

3. During the new-moon and full-moon ceremonies, a winnowing basket, a mortar and a pestle have to be placed on the western side of the sacred fire. The sacrificial food which is offered to the gods on the occasion has also to be placed on the western side.

4. For the ancestor-propitiation ceremony as also for the rites for protection from serpents, a mortar in which paddy is ritually husked

is placed to the west. But, as mentioned earlier, the husking of paddy for these rituals is done by placing the left hand above the right.

5. If a cow is being sacrificed in a rite sacred to ancestors, then its head should be towards the south and feet towards the west.

6. The entrance of one's house should not face the west.

South

1. During the morning and evening oblations the offerings to ancestors are placed on the southern side of the fire. The same is true of the offerings made to ancestors during the ancestor-propitiation ceremony.

2. For the ancestor-propitiation ceremony some *durva* grass which has been cut from the roots is strewn round the sacred fire. The blades of grass should point towards the south.

3. During the tonsure ceremony the ritual implements (brass vessel with hot water, a razor made of wood, and the metal razor which the barber is to use later) are placed towards the south of the fire but the hair that is shaved is thrown on a heap of cow-dung which is on the northern side of the fire. After the child's head has been shaved the hair is taken away to be buried or thrown into flowing water in a northerly direction.

4. The cow which is sacrificed during the rites to ancestors has its head towards the south and feet towards the west.

5. During the ancestor-propitiation ceremony the sacrificer draws a line from north to south and recites a formula saying, 'The *asuras* [demons] have been driven away'.

6. A person who is desirous of children, cattle, and fame should build his house so that it faces the southern direction. However, the Palasha tree which is associated with Yama (god of death) should not be planted towards the southern side as this entails danger of death.

This detailed enumeration of the contexts in which the different cardinal directions are made use of shows that east and north are associated with those rituals in which the right dominates, and south and west with those in which the left dominates. The rule that a cow being sacrificed to the gods should have its face towards the east and feet towards the north while in the case of a cow being sacrificed to ancestors, the face should be towards the south and feet towards the west, makes this association explicitly. The other rules also are consistent on this point. For instance, while preparing the sacred site for rites to gods, lines have to be drawn from west to east, and from south to north. Thus east and north are the directions *towards* which movement takes place in these rituals. The grass which is strewn round the sacred fire for these occasions either points towards the east or towards the north. Within the general category of rituals in which the right side dominates, a symbolic distinction is made between rites to mark the passage of time (e.g. morning, evening, advent of new-moon, full-moon, etc.) and rites to mark the passage from one status to another (e.g. marriage, pregnancy, childbirth). In the former rituals the grass strewn round the fire points towards the east and in the latter case towards the north. At the conclusion of any of these rites, the subject goes either in the eastern or the northern direction.

West is the direction which is associated with both ancestors and prosperity/fertility. Its association with ancestors is shown by the rule according to which the entrance to the enclosure, in which the ancestor-propitiation ceremony is held, is made towards the west. Significantly, since ancestors enter the world of the living during specified periods when they are propitiated, from the west, ordinary mortals are not allowed to use the same direction for entry. Hence the rule that a house should not have its entrance towards the west. The western direction is also associated with material prosperity and fertility of women. This is the side in which symbols of agricultural prosperity such as winnowing basket, mortar and pestle for husking paddy are placed. Also, at the rituals of marriage, pregnancy, and childbirth, the bride, the pregnant woman and the mother, respectively, sit on the western side of the fire. In view of the earlier analysis of the association of ancestors/other deities of the left with the power to bestow wealth and progeny on their descendants, it is not surprising to find that the direction in which symbols of prosperity and fertility are placed is also the direction from which ancestors enter to receive their share from their descendants. Thus the western side is associated with the benevolent aspect of ancestors and other deities of the left.

The southern direction is associated with death. The injunction that the Palasha tree which is associated with Yama should not be planted on the southern side of the house as this produces danger of death derives from this association. Correspondingly, south is associated with demons and other evil beings. Thus there are rules in which the *durva* grass is thrown from the north to the south, or a line is drawn from the north to the south, driving away Asuras, 'dispellers of wealth', demons and other evil beings. In the ancestor-propitiation ceremony the householder first drives away these evil beings and then invites his ancestors to accept his offerings. The sacrificial offerings to ancestors, serpents, and other deities of the left are always placed facing the southern direction. Thus south is the side in which the sacred beings associated with death such as serpents, ancestors, demons, and other left hand deities live. Along with the left side, the south is the cardinal point which figures in all rituals in which the danger emanating from these sacred beings has to be neutralized. It is in this context that one can understand why, during the tonsure ceremony, the barber and the other persons who officiate at the ritual are on the south and *durva* grass is pressed on the child's head with the left hand. Since the hair which a child had in the womb is considered to be a particularly apt object with which magical spells can be worked to harm the child, the left hand has to deal with this danger.[1] The hair is thrown on a heap of cow-dung to the north, symbolically assuring the child's welfare and his progress in life. Thus, along with the right side, the east and the north figure in rituals in which the life-processes and the good-sacred dominate and the left along with south figure in rituals in which death, magic, sorcery, and generally the bad-sacred dominates. West, as we have already pointed out, represents the harnessing of the left hand deities and ancestors for the welfare of their descendants and devotees.

The analysis of the means by which space is categorized shows that in association with the symbolism of laterality, the cardinal points provide symbols for representing different types of movements—the movement of time, the passage from one social status to another, especially connected with the continuation of the household through proper channelling of the forces of fertility and representation of death as a passage from the status of a living human being to that of an ancestor. (Cf. Leach, 1968; Rigby, 1968.) This is why so much emphasis is placed in the domestic ceremonies on ritualizing the advent of the new-moon and full-moon, the events connected with fertility such as marriage and childbirth and, finally, the ritualization of death. In this Hindu ritual does not seem to be different from other systems of ritual.

Conclusion

This section attempts to show the relevance of this analysis which is

[1] We would like to record our observation that the clothes and the hair of the child who has not undergone the tonsure ceremony are protected with great care as his life can be endangered if these are used in magical spells.

based on a literary text for understanding certain structural aspects of Hindu society. In particular it shall be argued that the structural categories which were found in the analysis of domestic ceremonies are not unique to the text which has been analysed. In fact variants of this pattern are found to be repeated in various field studies of Hinduism.

Srinivas's study of the Coorg rituals (Srinivas, 1952), which is rightly regarded as a classic, uses two different models for analysis of Hinduism. One is the model based on the opposition between sanskritic and non-sanskritic Hinduism, which in turn is related to his concept of spread. The other, and the more important, model is the general one which is based on the opposition between good-sacred and bad-sacred.

As an example of how Srinivas uses the sanskritic/non-sanskritic opposition let us consider the mode of ancestor-propitiation among the Coorgs. According to Srinivas, the Coorgs observe ancestor-propitiation by sacrificing pigs and fowls to ancestors. The sacrificial offerings consist of meat and liquor, and the officiating priests and oracles are members of some lower castes like the Banias. Also on other ceremonial occasions like harvest-festival and marriage, ancestors are offered some rice and meat curry. Ancestors are usually represented by rough unhewn stones, which incidentally also represent deities like Mari (smallpox goddess) and Nata (cobra). Srinivas calls this mode of propitiation non-sanskritic and notes that in the sanskritic mode of propitiation, as among the Brahman castes, the offerings consist not of meat but of balls of rice called *pinda*. He remarks:

Both the sanskritic and non-sanskritic modes of propitiation exist cheek by jowl as far as the bulk of the Coorgs are concerned. The more inquiring of men see the two modes of propitiation as mutually inconsistent but such an inconsistency does not seriously trouble anyone. All over India, sanskritic and non-sanskritic customs, often involving beliefs regarded as mutually inconsistent, are found existing together [Srinivas, 1952: 118].

Thus Srinivas's conceptual scheme consists of two mutually opposed systems, 'sanskritic' and 'non-sanskritic', and any one ceremony is made up of an aggregation of traits from both systems. The higher castes, according to this scheme, have a greater proportion of sanskritic traits in their rituals while the lower castes have a greater proportion of non-sanskritic traits. It seems to us that the analytical inadequacy of this scheme lies in the fact that it conceptualizes a system as an aggregation of traits and hence lays itself open to the charge of atomization. The basic isolates in this scheme are elements and not relations. Further, Srinivas does not construct any models of the systems that he calls sanskritic and non-sanskritic. Even if these terms were adequate for purposes of description, which, given the heterogeneity of ritual and belief covered under these terms, they are not, little would be gained by substituting one set of descriptive terms (the offering of meat and liquor on the occasion of ancestor-propitation, representation of ancestors through crude, unhewn stones, etc.) by another, e.g. non-sanskritic, mode of ancestor-propitiation.

It may, of course, be argued that the utility of a term like sanskritization lies in the fact that people themselves attribute greater value to sanskritic values as they conceive these to be. The argument has some weight if we confine ourselves to a limited temporal framework. If we take a larger canvas of time, then the relevant question is not why the Coorgs do not see any contradiction between claiming to be Kshatriyas and offering meat to ancestors, but how the Brahmans substituted rice-offerings for the textually prescribed meat-offerings to ancestors and continued to call these *pinda*. In order to understand this problem we would need to assess the impact of Vaishnava movements on the life-styles of Brahman castes which, as has been earlier argued, requires an inquiry into the relations between the institutions of kingship, caste and sect in the Indian context. It has already been shown in an earlier chapter that Brahmans in the medieval period were characterized as those who consumed meat and liquor, and offered it in their sacrifices, and that the changes in the life-styles of the Brahmans may be traced to their position as mediators between the 'renouncer' and the 'man-in-the-world'. The important point is that in understanding a society like India with a long and continuous civilization our problems cannot be defined in a narrow spatio-temporal framework, since a consideration of the historical processes is likely to change the very way in which we formulate our problems of enquiry.

The second model which Srinivas uses, and which is based on the opposition of good-sacred and bad-sacred, seems to be more useful in dealing with Coorg rituals. Given the universality of the fact that margins or liminal states (Douglas, 1966; Turner, 1969) are seen as dangerous in every society and hence become subjects of taboo, ritual and myth, one can expect that rites of passage will occupy an important place in the ritual life of the people. However, a distinction must be made between the states of marginality associated with life-processes (e.g. marriage and childbirth) and the state of liminality associated with death. Events and persons associated with death are seen as imbued with danger, and an important part of ritual life consists in neutralizing this danger arising out of the fact of death. Among the Coorgs we find that there is an identity in the symbols which represent deities, like the cobra deity, the smallpox goddess, and ancestors. These are not only represented by unhewn stones, but are even placed together in the ancestor shrine or on an earthen platform during the ancestor-propitiation ceremony. It is as if the danger which is constantly present in the form of cobras or epidemics is neutralized by propitiating these deities and ancestors simultaneously. It is difficult to determine whether a term like 'bad-sacred' is really adequate in dealing with this complex. Ancestors are not negatively sacred, as for instance the Devil is in Christian theology. The rituals associated with ancestors, cobras and the deities of various epidemics seem to be directed towards neutralizing the dangers emanating from the fact of death at the intellectual, religious and emotional levels. In fact the next chapter attempts to show that it is much more useful to divide the sacred in terms of the opposition of life and death, rather than in terms of the opposition of good and bad. At least in Hindu cosmology the sacred is seen much more usefully as ordered with reference to life-death opposition than good-bad opposition.

The states of marginality associated with life-processes are also linked with ideas of danger. However, in this case the danger is *to* the person who is in the liminal state—the new-born baby, the bride, and the new mother. The mode of propitiating ancestors with offerings of meat and liquor should be understood in opposition to the mode of propitiating deities who preside over liminal states in the life-processes, with offerings of vegetables and grain. We have already seen how the opposition between meat and vegetables is associated with a number of other oppositions in the Grihya Sutra. Taken together, these series of antithetical pairs express the duality of the two types of liminality that we have mentioned above. To tie up the analysis of Hindu ritual to variations in caste as the sanskritic/non-sanskritic model does, will not help in the analytical task, though Srinivas does seem to have been more attracted to this model later for an understanding of Hindu religion (cf. Srinivas & Shah, 1968).

In this context Dumont's views should be briefly considered. He has argued for the encompassing nature of the pure/impure opposition in Hinduism as against the sacred/profane opposition elsewhere (Dumont, 1970a). Dumont maintains that Hindu society differs from other societies, in that events such as death which are seen as imbued with danger in other societies are seen as involving only impurity in India. Thus the central structural feature of Hindu society for Dumont is the opposition between the pure and the impure. This opposition, according to him, is not only manifest in the social order but also in the sacred order. He demonstrates this by an analysis of the characteristics of Aiyanar, a folk deity in Tamil villages. There is some variation in the characteristics of Aiyanar in different villages in Tamilnadu. According to the myths surrounding his origin, he was born of the gods Shiva and Vishnu, when the latter had assumed a female form to beguile the demons. Aiyanar is sometimes described as the king of demons. He is often associated with various village goddesses, whose essential function is to protect the village against epidemics and the principal goddess among these is Mariyamman, the smallpox goddess. Aiyanar is also associated with Ka-Ruppan, locally known as the Black god in the lineage pantheon of some castes, such as the Pramalai Kallar on whom Dumont relies heavily. Here he appears as a vegetarian god, opposed to the meat-eating, dark god Karrupu. Describing the lineage temples, Dumont says that the temple is divided between meat-eating gods and vegetarian gods. The former are placed to the south, the latter to the north. The priests for the two are different: the former having the 'little' priest for officiating and the latter having the 'great' priest. However, the existence of both types of gods is seen as regular and necessary. Dumont relates the story of a man who is terribly confused because both the non-vegetarian and the vegetarian gods are incarnate in him and the confusion is only resolved when an arbitrator ascribes the right side to the vegetarian god and the left to the non-vegetarian god.

In analysing the lineage pantheon, Dumont argues that the sacred order has to be understood in relation to the social order. Therefore the relation between vegetarian and meat-eating gods is the same as the relation between vegetarian and meat-eating men, which is that of superiors to inferiors. Thus the distinction between the two types of gods is a particular form of the opposition of purity and impurity which is the principle of the caste system. Since the Pramalai Kallar are meat-eating they offer the gods with whom they identify themselves meat and blood-sacrifices. Incidentally, this is the same explanation that Srinivas offered for blood-sacrifices and offerings of meat to ancestors among the Coorgs. However, Dumont is still faced with the problem of explaining the presence of the vegetarian gods in the temples of meat-eating gods. In this context Dumont (1970: 28) argues that ' . . . in the last analysis the pure god is not present in the temple by virtue of his intrinsic superiority, but as *the god of the superior castes*. It would appear as if the caste joins to its own gods those of the castes that dominate it. *Here we have to substitute a psychology of imitation for a psychology of conversion*' (emphasis added). Thus Dumont's structuralism has to give way to a theory based on dubious psychology and the pantheon is seen as an *aggregation of traits* and not as a structural entity. To the meat-eating god with whom the Pramalai Kallars identify themselves are added the vegetarian gods of the higher castes whom the Kallars wish to imitate.

As we have suggested earlier, the relation between ancestors, lineage-gods, and deities representing smallpox, the cobra, etc. can be seen in their association with death rather than in their association with impurity. Thus it seems that the association of the left with liminal states associated with death and the reservation of the south for ancestors and other deities is not confined to the text which we have analysed. In fact there appear to be remarkable constancies in the meaning of the right and left sides, as also in the categorization of space, whether one analyses lineage-pantheons, rites of passage, folk-myths or any other aspect of the religious life of the people. The strongest reason for taking up serious analyses of such texts is that the variants of the structure which we analyse from these texts are found to be repeated in the rituals and beliefs of different social groups among Hindus today. It is here that the justification for treating Hinduism as a system is to be found. Any theory, whether it is based on the opposition of the sanskritic and the non-sanskritic or on the opposition between the pure and the impure, which ends up by treating Hinduism as a random juxtaposition of traits needs to be seriously reconsidered.

5

The Sacred and the Profane in Hinduism

I

IN THE last chapter it was argued that the ordering of the sacred in Hinduism differs from that proposed by Durkheim, in that the sacred was seen as divided with reference to the opposition of life and death rather than good and bad. In order to understand the significance of this argument it is necessary now to relate it to existing formulations about the ordering of the sacred in Hindu belief and ritual. Three major arguments that have been proposed on these issues will be discussed here. The first is that the dichotomy of sacred and profane which dominated the Durkheimian sociology of religion has very little relevance in the Hindu context, since these are not antithetical in Hindu belief and ritual (see Inden and Nicholas, 1977). The second formulation follows that of Durkheim and accepts the dichotomy of the sacred and the profane, dividing the sacred into good-sacred and bad-sacred. Srinivas (1952), who elaborated this model in his study of the Coorgs, associated purity with good-sacredness and impurity with bad-sacredness. He also argued that pure and impure were hierarchically ordered and characterized the normal ritual status as that of mild impurity. The third formulation is that of Dumont, who argued that events which are seen as imbued with danger in other societies incur pollution in Hindu society. Dumont's formulation of the relation between the two dichotomies of sacred/profane and pure/impure altered over the years. In his essay 'Pure and Impure', he contended that the dichotomy of the sacred and the profane was operative at the cosmic level, and the dichotomy of pure and impure at the social level. However, he went on to say that 'the religion of gods is secondary, and the religion of caste is fundamental' (Dumont and Pocock, 1959: 34). But his later contention (1971) was that the relation between sacred, pure and impure could be seen as one in which each preceding term encompassed the latter ones. He did not care to comment on the apparent contradiction between these two formulations. In the following discussion we shall show the relevance of the sacred/profane dichotomy and its internal ordering in terms of the opposition of life and death. Finally, it will be shown that the symbolism of impurity serves basically as a metaphor for liminality.

II

Durkheim's distinction between the sacred and the profane has come under sharp attack from those who expected to find a division of all things into these two mutually exclusive, antithetical categories at the level of the empirical reality. For instance, Stanner (1967) reports his distress at not being able to apply this distinction to all actions and beliefs of the aborigines in the course of his fieldwork among the Mwaimkatta. Similarly, Inden and Nicholas (1977) seem to imply that the sacred impinges on the profane so deeply in Hindu social life that there is little meaning in insisting on distinguishing one from the other. This is, to a large extent, a restatement of the view that Hinduism is not a religion but a way of life.

It would seem that much of the confusion in discussions of the sacred/profane dichotomy has arisen because Stanner and others have reduced it to an empirical dichotomy. To some extent, Durkheim himself contributed to this confusion. The concept of sacred, however, seems too fundamental to be discarded simply because it cannot serve as an efficient tool of observation. In distinguishing the sacred from the profane, Durkheim was trying to resolve a fundamental philosophical problem about the nature of social order. It is well known that before he wrote *The Elementary Forms of the Religious Life* (1964) he found it difficult to resolve the problem of the stability of the social order as in his earlier work he had placed too great an emphasis on the criterion of formal obligation. With the concept of the sacred he was able to demonstrate that social control must flow from the axiology of social life and not from the stress on formal obligation. Thus, the concept of the sacred allowed Durkheim to distinguish between society as a mere balance of power between groups and individuals, and society as a moral community. The 'morality' of a society lies in the system of meanings within which it locates human existence and which it accepts as being axiomatically true.

It is interesting to note that, in some form or other, emphasis on the axiomatic character of society came to be placed by those philosophers who were trying to react against the social contract theory of social order. For instance, Whitehead (1958) attributed the stability of a social order to collective prejudices of a society. Though the term 'prejudices' implies a value-judgement, Whitehead seems to imply that these commonly shared sentiments are above considerations of rationality, efficiency and mutual adjustment of interests.

The same concern in distinguishing religious discourse from other kinds of discourse is evident in Wittgenstein (1966). He also seems to suggest that religious discourse belongs to an altogether different plane; religious beliefs are marked by an axiomatic character and are, therefore, characterized by words like 'faith' or 'dogma' rather than 'opinion' or 'view'. The following quotations from his conversations can be seen to express these ideas:

Suppose someone were a believer and said: 'I believe in a Last Judgement' and I said: 'Well, I am not so sure. Possibly.' You would say that there is an enormous gulf between us. If he said, 'There is a German aeroplane overhead', and I said, 'Possibly, I am not sure', you would say we were fairly near.

It isn't a question of my being anywhere near him, but on an entirely different plane. . . [p. 53].

In another place he remarks,

This is why one would be reluctant to say: 'These people rigorously hold the opinion (or view) that there is a Last Judgement.' Opinion sounds queer.

It is for this reason that different words are used: 'dogma', 'faith' [p. 57].

Thus, the concept of the sacred, as Durkheim conceived it, separates the domain of religious discourse from other types of discourse and bestows society with an axiomatic, 'taken-for-granted' cognitive quality. The historicially crucial part of religion in legitimizing the particular institutions of a society as axiomatic is best explained in terms of its unique capacity to 'locate' human phenomena within a cosmic frame of reference. This process of cosmization endows the inherently precarious and transitory constructions of human activity with a security, durability and permanence, which takes on an axiomatic character (see Berger, 1969). It is, however, not only in Hinduism but also in such religions as Islam and Christianity that particular social institutions and roles are incorporated within a sacred design. For instance, Islamic law which regulates so many profane activities of a Muslim is essentially religious law. Similarly, the notions of Christian conduct, Christian marriage, etc. point to the fact that it is not only Hinduism but also Christianity which is conceived as a way of life. The location of human institutions within a sacred, cosmic design is not evidence of the inadequacy of the concept of sacred, but rather of its all-encompassing nature.

It is obvious, therefore, that the difficulties faced in distinguishing the sacred from the profane at the empirical level do not provide sufficient grounds for rejecting the dichotomy. The distinction is heuristically important as long as there is a need to endow society with an axiomatic, taken-for-granted cognitive quality. Nevertheless, Stanner's discomfort at not being able to reconcile Van Gennep's (1960) theory of the rites of passage with the Durkheimian division of the universe into the sacred and the profane seems real. We shall, therefore, examine the implications of Van Gennep's theory for Durkheim's sociology of religion, especially as this will help us later in understanding rules of impurity within the framework of the sacred proposed here.

There is clear evidence in *The Elementary Forms of the Religious Life* (1964) that Durkheim saw the social order as continuously threatened by individual, profane interests. Hence, when he emphasized the integrative function of ritual he clearly recognized that the shared system of meanings in a society, though having an axiomatic quality, had to be recreated again and again in each individual consciousness through the common enactment of ritual. It seems preferable to understand his argument about the integrative function of rituals in this sense rather than in terms of a theory of crowd psychology.

Van Gennep's theory of the rites of passage went further than Durkheim's in that, beyond the threat of interests, Van Gennep emphasized the threatening nature of all liminalities—intellectual, social, and cosmic. He pointed out that being unclassifiable, these liminalities have the potential of disrupting the particular classifications imposed by man on his given reality. In this sense, as Berger (1969) says, every system of reality is threatened by lurking 'irrealities' and every mode of being is threatened by the ultimate state of non-being.

9

While Durkheim was aware that the social order, constructed and maintained by the sacred, was precariously balanced, he thought that its precariousness stemmed from the threat of individual, profane *interests*. Following Van Gennep, we now realize that religion has to provide not only an all-encompassing sacred order which can transform the empirical tenuousness of institutions by placing them within a cosmic order, but it also has to devise ways and means by which the liminalities experienced by an individual can be dealt with without any loss of meaning.

Durkheim recognized the ambiguities in the concept of the sacred in his analysis of piacular rites. Thus, while he maintained that the sacred always appears as extraordinary and potentially dangerous, though, as Hertz (1960) argued, its dangers can be domesticated, he was emphatic that the distinction between the sacred and the profane was not equivalent to the distinction between good and bad. As Durkheim argued, the sacred can be evil and eminently so. He divided the sacred itself into the good-sacred and the bad-sacred, both of which retained the quality of 'sticking out' from the world of the non-sacred. It is our contention here that it was in assigning a universal division of the sacred into 'good' and 'bad' that Durkheim tended to elevate the categories of a particular culture to the level of universal, analytical categories.

Not all the followers of the *Année Sociologique* school were happy with this ordering of the sacred. For instance, Hertz (1960) used the term 'profane' in much the same sense as Durkheim would have used the term 'negative sacredness', when he designated the functions of the left hand as those dealing with the profane. In this Hertz was closer to medieval Christianity, for the 'bad-sacred' activities of Satan and his followers consist primarily of profaning the sacred by black-mass, reading the Bible backwards, wearing the cross upside down and so on. More recently, Dumont (1971:75) has expressed his dissatisfaction with the term 'bad-sacred'. Dumont considers it a contradiction in terms. Others have argued that in the Indian case they prefer to use relative and sliding terms such as 'more sacred' and 'less sacred' rather than the absolute distinction of dividing the sacred into good and bad. Srinivas (1952) had a similar argument for conceptualizing the pure and impure as 'relatively pure' and 'relatively impure', designating the normal ritual status as that of mild impurity. We would suggest that the difficulties which Dumont and Beck point out arise through a failure to see that the sacred may be divided and ordered with reference to different kinds of oppositions. It would be readily conceded that whatever the ultimate nature of sacred experiences, for our purpose the sacred is essentially a human construction. As such, it has to be analysed as all other products of human activity, that is, as a cultural projection which men make in order to superimpose a system of meanings on their experience. It follows from this that just as the historical manifestations of the sacred vary widely, so may we expect that the particular ordering of the sacred will also vary historically and cross-culturally.

The analysis of the data on domestic rituals strongly suggests that the sacred in Hindu belief and ritual should be conceptualized as divided with reference to the opposition of life and death rather than the opposition of good and bad, as in Srinivas (1952). The right side dominates events associated with life, such as pregnancy, blessing of a new-born child, marriage and initiation, through which contact is established between man and the sacred associated with life. On the other hand, cremation, propitiation of ancestors and worship of deities associated with death and destruction are events which entail the establishment of contact between man and the forces of the sacred associated with death, dominated by the left.

Schematically the argument may be represented as follows:

Rituals associated with the use of right	*Rituals associated with the use of left*
1 Passage of time	1 Death rituals
2 Rites of initiation	2 Rites to ghosts, demons, etc.
3 Rites of pregnancy	3 Rites to ancestors
4 Rites of marriage	4 Rites to serpents

It can be seen immediately from this schematic representation that the opposition of right and left, as argued earlier, is not equivalent to the opposition of pure and impure. The events from which an individual incurs impurity cut across this division. Thus, while the pregnant woman and the new mother are both subjects of ritual in which the right side dominates, it is only childbirth and not pregnancy which involves impurity. Similarly, the left side dominates in cremation rituals as well as in the propitiation of ancestors; yet the former is associated with impurity but not the latter. Thus, it seems that the state of purity is considered appropriate in dealing with the cosmic when it is experienced as integrated with the social, as in daily prayer, rites to ancestors, etc. On the other hand, the symbolism of impurity marks off situations which are liminal in the sense that the individual experiences his social world as separated from the cosmic. The paradigm for liminality is provided by death and the contrast between the *preta* (ghost) and *pitri* (ancestor) in death rituals brings out clearly the difference between these two types of relationships between the cosmic and the social. For this reason, the death rituals will be discussed in some detail in this chapter. We hope to show that, at one level, the sacred associated with life is kept completely separate from the sacred associated with death, as in the injunction that no weddings should be performed in the month of *shradha* when ancestors are propitiated. At another level, there is a difference between rituals associated with the propitiation of ancestors and rituals associated with cremation. Though there is a dominance of the left side in both cases, in the former case one is dealing with categories (e.g. ancestors) which do not disturb the cosmization of social reality. On the other hand, every death (or birth) has to be legitimized by being integrated with the microcosmic/macrocosmic system of social and cosmic reality. The whole purpose of ritual in these cases is to define death away from an accidental, contingent event to one which is part of a cosmic design. In other words, while ancestors (*pitri*) as a category are already integrated with cosmic reality, a dead man as ghost (*preta*) is a liminal category and has to be converted into the incorporated category of ancestor. It will be shown now that rules of impurity incurred at death basically serve as a metaphor for liminality.

III

An impressive body of literature has grown in recent years showing the threat of liminality in all societies. The events associated with liminal positions are ritualized, dramatized or glossed over by the use of linguistic euphemisms. (See Douglas, 1966; Leach, 1969; Turner, 1962.) The profound threat of these liminal positions lies in their power to question the ordering of everyday reality, through their capacity to ignore or transcend normal customary divisions. Of all the liminal positions in a society, those in which the individual experiences his social and cosmic world as dissociated are especially potent. The paradigm of liminality *par excellence* is death. It is, as Berger (1969) argues, not only that death poses an obvious threat to the continuity of human relationships but also that it threatens the basic assumption of order on which human society rests. The severe impurity which mourners incur on death and the taboos associated with its occurrence are expressive of the liminality of this event. In Hindu religious thought death releases the individual soul, enabling it to penetrate the world of illusion (*maya*) and return to the true and eternal Brahman. Thus, the act of dying is a very significant act for a Hindu. Hindu scriptures enjoin upon the individual the duty of preparation for death and the preservation of the purity of body and spirit. Yet, the only aspect of death which has received some attention in anthropological literature is the attendant pollution of the mourners and the ritual procedures for its removal. We propose to analyse the themes pertaining to death in somewhat greater detail here, drawing the data from the *Garuda Purana, Krityakalpataru* of Bhatta Sri Laksmidhara and *Antyestisamskara* of Narayanabhatta. Where possible, the ritual injunctions given in the texts will be compared with the available ethnographies, such as Srinivas (1952), Stevenson (1971) and Kaushik (1976).

In describing the method of cremating the dead body, it is said in the *Garuda Purana* that if a son cremates the body of his father in accordance with proper ritual procedure, he accumulates merit equal to that achieved by offering several *danas*. Hence, the son is enjoined to overcome his grief and to prepare himself for the performance of the rituals by getting his head shaved, bathing, and wearing wet clothes. It is prescribed that for performance of death rituals the mourner should wear the sacred thread over his right shoulder so that it hangs towards his left side. This mode of wearing the sacred thread is prescribed for all occasions in which a person makes contact with the sacred associated with death, e.g. in cremation rituals, rites to ancestors, etc.

The dead body is bathed, dressed in new clothes, rubbed with sandalwood, and decked with flowers. The orifices are cleansed of all faecal matter and are required to be stuffed with clarified butter and sandalwood paste. A married woman is decked like a bride. The corpse is referred to as Shiva in the *Garuda Purana*, as when the widow is told that she should consider the corpse of her husband to be Shiva. Stevenson (1971) also reports that the corpse of a male is referred to as Vishnu and the corpse of a female as Lakshmi. All the people in the house are required to circumambulate the corpse in the auspicious direction, e.g. with their right sides towards the corpse. It should be noted that in contrast the corpse is circumambulated with the left side towards it when it is laid on the pyre in the cremation ground.

The corpse is guarded in various ways from unclean or impure objects. Stevenson (1971) reports that great care is taken to guard the 'holy body' from the approach of unclean animals such as cats, for 'its merest touch would pollute the sacred corpse'. The *Garuda Purana* also emphasizes that the *preta* (ghost) which is imprisoned within the body is in great danger from various types of demons and these have to be appeased by a series of *pinda dana*, all along the way to the cremation ground.

At the cremation ground, an appropriate place is prepared for the pyre. This place has first to be swept, then smeared with the purifying cow-dung and appropriate lines drawn on the ground with the sacred *kusa* grass. As in all fire-sacrifices, the *vedi* (altar) is established within these lines. After consecrating the *vedi* with holy water, Agni (the fire-god) is established in the *vedi*. He is worshipped with flowers and water, and a fire-sacrifice is performed to the chant of the proper *mantras* (sacred formulae). The theme of these *mantras* is a request to Agni to accept the dead man and carry him to heaven.

After Agni, the fire-god, has been properly worshipped, a pyre is made with the ritually prescribed woods, such as sandalwood, *tulasi* (Basil) and *pippala* (*Ficus religiosa*). Before being placed on the pyre the body is washed with the holy water of the Ganga. The mourners are expected to ensure that cremation does not take place during the inauspicious period of *panchaka*, and if it becomes necessary to cremate the body during the inauspicious period then further expiatory rituals become necessary.

After the cremation, a series of further offerings to the *preta* (ghost) are prescribed. The final offering, as is well known, is the one in which the *sapindikarana* (making of same substance) of the *preta* takes place and he becomes incorporated with the *pitri* (ancestors).

The description seems to suggest that one important theme in the death-ritual is the offering of the dead man, through a sacrifice to the gods and ancestors. Stevenson (1971) explicitly states that the dead man is seen as an offering to Agni. If we recall the basic elements in the scheme of a sacrifice, outlined by Hubert and Mauss (1964), we find striking similarities with the cremation rituals. Thus the site of cremation is prepared in exactly the same manner as in fire-sacrifice, i.e. the prescriptive use of ritually pure wood, the purifica-

tion of the site, its consecration with holy water, and the establishment of Agni with the use of proper *mantras*. The time chosen for
cremation has to be an auspicious one. The dead body is prepared in
the same manner as the victim of a sacrifice and is attributed with
divinity. Just as the victim of a sacrifice is exhorted not to take any
revenge for the pains which the sacrifice has inflicted on him (Hubert
& Mauss, 1964) so the mourners pray to the *preta* to spare them
from his anger at the burns he has suffered in the fire (*Garuda Purana*).
The successful completion of the death rituals ensures that the spirit
of the dead man merges with the cosmic forces. As in other sacrifices,
the sacrificer, who is the son in this case, achieves religious merit
through having performed the sacrificial rituals in accordance with
prescribed procedures. It would appear that the attention which has
hitherto been paid to the condition of the mourners in sociological
analyses of death in Hinduism, to the exclusion of the condition of
the corpse, has obscured the importance of sacrifice as a theme in
Hindu mortuary rituals.

It is significant that in cases of sudden death, unnatural death, or
in the case of sinners when either a person is not deemed fit to be a
sacrificial object or where a person's intention to sacrifice himself
through death is not established, the person is not allowed to be
cremated. Similarly, in the case of victims of such diseases as smallpox, when death is seen as an offering to the wrath of the *mata*
(mother goddess), cremation does not take place. In the case of an
ascetic too, his *tapa* is said to burn him internally so that he also is
not cremated. Whereas several explanations may be given about these
exceptions, e.g. in terms of the hot/cold opposition as in Kaushik
(1976), or in terms of the double obsequies (Hertz, 1960), we believe
our interpretation enables us to include all the exceptions into a
single class of people consisting of those whose intention to sacrifice
themselves through death is not established, as in the case of children
and victims of sudden death; those who are not fit sacrificial objects
such as sinners; and those whose death may be seen as an indication
of their having already been offered to the gods. Gandhi, steeped in
the tenets of Hindu religion, once remarked that he wished to lead a
pure life so that in death he would not be rejected by the gods.

The theme of sacrifice, which we have suggested is a major one in
death, seems somewhat incompatible with the idea that the corpse
is impure. Yet various texts, including the *Krityakalpataru*, endow the
corpse with such severe impurity that it has to be destroyed. The con-

tradition, however, is perhaps more apparent than real. It is significant that the corpse is not referred to by a single term in all contexts. For instance, in the *Shuddhi Kanda* of *Krityakalpataru* the corpse is referred to as *kunapa* in contexts where its impurity is being discussed. On the other hand, rites performed at death are known as *pretasamskara*, rites to the *preta* (ghost). Similarly in instructions on how the corpse should be carried, it is referred to as the *preta*. The common belief is that immediately on his death, the spirit of a man takes on the existence of a ghost (*preta*). If a person has led a pure life, this period of his existence is a transitory one. He is acceptable as a sacrifice to the gods and ancestors and through their acceptance becomes incorporated as an ancestor. His incorporation in the world of ancestors also depends upon the correct performance of rituals and the proper observance of taboos by the mourners.

The point is that the *preta* is seen as trapped in the skull of the dead man. It is released only when the chief mourner breaks the skull of the half-cremated body. At this stage the ritual fire (*agni*), which has in his own lifetime carried the ritual offerings to the gods, carries him as an offering to the god of death and ancestors. The fact that the *preta* is trapped in the body—indeed, the corpse is referred to as the *preta*—explains its treatment as a sacrificial object. However, the corpse is also the matter which the spirit leaves behind. This matter is impure and we believe that when the corpse is described as impure it is to the corpse as matter and not to the corpse as *preta* that reference is being made. The sacrificial fire simultaneously destroys the corpse as matter and carries the spirit of the man upwards to the god of death and ancestors.

The dead man remains a *preta* for a period ranging from ten to thirty days, depending upon his caste. After this period, if the rituals have been performed correctly, he becomes incorporated among the ancestors. This incorporation is symbolized by the crucial rites of *sapindikarana*, which convert the *preta* to a *pitri* (ancestor). Henceforth the householder is enjoined to propitiate him as an ancestor on prescribed occasions. His incorporation as an ancestor symbolizes the acceptance of the offering made of the dead man, and he is said to have achieved *sadgati*, a good end, as opposed to *durgati*, a bad end, which is reserved for ghosts and demons. The *preta* of the victims of unnatural deaths and of sinners is not incorporated and is doomed to permanent liminality.

Let us now examine the condition of the mourners. Death is said to be a source of severe impurity for the living kinsmen of the deceased. Of all the mourners, the chief-mourner who lights the funeral pyre is the subject of special taboos. The mourners are required to desist from shaving, combing hair, using footwear and cosmetics. They are also expected to eat only bland and unspiced food, sleep on the floor and wear white, unbleached clothes. Married women are not allowed to use *sindoor* in the parting of their hair (see Kaushik, 1976). The impurity of death begins the moment the *preta* is released from the body of the dead man. It gradually decreases with the passage of time. Different rituals mark successive terminations of the taboos on the different grades of mourners (see Srinivas, 1952; Dumont & Pocock, 1959). The impurity of the first grade mourners ends with the incorporation of the *preta* as *pitri*. After this, the first grade mourners re-enter the social world as bearers of new roles and statuses. Thus the widow of the dead man cannot make a re-entry as a wife. She is now incorporated into the social world as a widow and a host of taboos define her position.

It is clear that the impurity of death marks off the mourners till the liminal category of the *preta* has been converted into the incorporated category of the ancestor. This incorporation ensures that though the social relationship has been terminated by the fact of death, it continues within a cosmic framework. Thus ritual converts death from an accidental, contingent event capable of questioning the entire social order into a part of the design of a cosmic order. As Lévi-Strauss (1964: 216) says, 'Although experience contradicts theory, social life validates cosmology by its similarity of structure. Hence cosmology is true.'

The impurity of death marks off the mourners for the period when they are dealing with the liminal category of the *preta*; similarly, birth-impurity marks off the relatives of the new-born, till the child has been incorporated as a person, within the cosmic order. The rituals within the first forty days, the period for which the impurity of the mother and child lasts in most communities, emphasize the incorporation of the child as part of a cosmic design. For instance, on *sutika shashti*, six days after the birth of the child, he is ceremonially offered to the goddess Shasthi. On this day Brahma is said to come himself and write the future of the child. The rituals on these occasions have the dominant theme of presenting the child to the gods, and of the gods descending to write out the future of the child. Thus individual biography takes on the character of events ordained by gods. It is well known that the complete incorporation of the child in the social world only takes place with the initiation of the boy, and marriage of the girl. Therefore, more than symbolizing the emergence of the child as a complete social personality, the end of childbirth impurity symbolizes his incorporation within a cosmic design. This is why we have stressed the point that impurity symbolizes liminality; it marks off the events in which man experiences his social world as separate from the cosmic world. The termination of impurity in the case of both birth and death is coterminous with the incorporation of the social into the cosmic world, so that they are again experienced as integrated. We think that this is a much more satisfactory explanation than the one which traces these impurities to the incurring of pollution through bodily processes.

The taboos on the mourner, which we have described earlier, clearly have some similarity with the behaviour of the ascetic. The ban on shaving, combing hair, using footwear and the prescription to eat unspiced, bland food and sleep on the floor all point to an ascetic performance which is enjoined on the mourner. Dumont (1971) notes this similarity but fails to explain why an ascetic performance should be enjoined on the mourner for the removal of impurity. However, if we look at impurity as symbolizing liminality, then the similarity between the mourners and the ascetic is easy to explain. The ascetic transcends the categories of the social and the cosmic world. Similarly the mourner stands outside the system while he is dealing with a liminal cosmic category, that of the *preta*. The renouncer's liminality is permanent while the mourner returns to the social world with the incorporation of the *preta* with the *pitri*.

IV

In this section we would like to draw the attention of the reader to the use of body symbolism in defining impurity. Use of the body as a metaphor in the description of the social system is a recurrent theme in Hinduism. In the famous *Purusa Sukta*, which describes the origin of the four *varnas*, the body is divided horizontally and hierarchically, with the Brahmans emerging from the head, the Kshatriyas from the arms, the Vaishyas from the thighs and the Shudras from the feet of primeval man. The hierarchical division of the body serves as suitable metaphor for the hierarchical division of society into four *varnas*. In contrast, in the Grihya Sutras the body is divided laterally into two inverse and symmetrical parts. This mode of dividing the body is particularly apt for describing the division of the sacred with reference to the opposition of life and death.

In the case of the symbolism of impurity, it is the peripheries of the body which are emphasized. Thus hair and nails, which figure prominently in this, have a peripheral position in relation to the body as they can both belong to the body and yet be outside it. It is significant that both the hair and nails are allowed to grow in a natural state to symbolize impurity. Similarly the extremities are not constrained but are left free. The feet are not constrained by shoes. The hair is left open, neither combed nor tied by a turban. For married women, the *sindoor* normally divides the head into the right and the left sides but the use of *sindoor* for this division is not permitted. In the case of a widow, the hair is required to be cut in such a way that the parting is not visible. Similarly, in certain communities the wearing of rings (bangles, *payzebs*, etc.) which constrain the hands and the feet is forbidden during mourning.[1] The use of white, which is typically used to symbolize the absence of differentiation, also points to the liminal character of the mourners. Thus the body in its constrained state stands as a metaphor for the social system, representing the containment of categories. Play on hair, nails, and extremities allows the use of body symbolism to express both the normal containment of categories and a state of liminality. It seems to us that it is the body as a natural, unconstrained system which expressed liminality. The end of impurity is symbolized by shaving, combing the hair, putting on footwear and, for the male-mourners, the custom of tying the head with a turban. For women the normal parting of the hair is restored by the use of *sindoor* and they are again allowed to wear rings on their hands and feet. Thus the return of the mourners to normal social life is symbolized by the body as a bounded, cultural system (as distinct from a flowing, natural system) which symbolizes the containment of categories.

It is not surprising that witchcraft and magic should use the body as a natural, flowing system rather than the cultural, constrained one, for in its bounded position the body cannot be used for magical manipulation. Thus, witches are always represented with flowing hair and

---

[1] In some communities married women continue to wear glass bangles during the period of mourning. These are later broken to mark the end of mourning and new ones are worn. There seem to be considerable regional variations of this custom.

long nails. Similarly, body-secretions which by their very nature are ambiguous and have to be removed to end impurity, are used as potent elements in witchcraft, sorcery, and magical rituals. In this manner the particular taboos about hair, nails, footwear, etc. also use the body to express the liminal character of the symbolism of impurity.

Our interpretation of pure and impure above leads us to question the formulations of Dumont and Srinivas on two major issues, viz. the identification of the impurity incurred on birth and death with caste pollution, and the conceptualization of pure and impure as hierarchically arranged on a single continuum from severe impurity through lessening impurity to purity.

The identification of birth and death pollution with caste pollution seems fraught with many problems. First of all specific terms exist for birth pollution (*sutaka, jananasaucha*)[1] and death pollution (*maranasaucha*). Such terms are missing for caste pollution in some regions and in others the terms for 'untouchables' cannot be derived from birth and death pollution. For instance, untouchable castes may be referred to by such terms as *achhuta* (lit., not to be touched) in Hindi-speaking areas, but here the translation of the term *achhuta* by the term impure is a little imprecise. It is true that impurity may be referred to by the term *chhuta* but this refers to the mode by which impurity may be conveyed rather than to its nature. It may also be pointed out that in some regions, impurity incurred on birth or death is itself divided into 'auspicious impurity' and 'inauspicious impurity'. In Bengal, for instance, the impurity at birth is auspicious (*shubher asaucha*), while the impurity of death is inauspicious (*ashubher asaucha*). This makes the straightforward assimilation of pure into 'good-sacred' and impure into 'bad-sacred' difficult, as in Srinivas's (1952) formulation.

In addition to the semantic difficulties, the rules about variations in impurity incurred by members of different castes are difficult to explain if we posit on identity between the impurity incurred at birth and death, and caste impurity. It is well known that the impurity incurred at birth or death increases as we go down the *varna* hierarchy so that the Brahman is subject to the least pollution and the Shudra

---

[1] The term *sutaka* can also be used to refer to death impurity, but its association with birth impurity is stronger as becomes evident on an examination of other related terms. Thus the verb *su* means procreating, begetting, bringing forth; *sutri* refers to the female genitals, and *sutika* to a woman who has recently delivered.

incurs the maximum pollution (see Orenstein, 1968). Yet, in the conduct of his daily affairs such as eating, it is the Brahman who is most vulnerable to pollution and has to protect himself ever from the sight of polluting persons such as untouchables, eunuchs, dogs, etc. Thus the Hindu may enter pure or impure states in relation to both the sacred and non-sacred (profane), but it is a mistake to treat these as identical. The 'purity' of a person who is offering prayer is quali- tatively different from the normal 'impurity' of the non-sacred state.[1]

The data on death-impurity presented in this chapter makes it difficult to conceptualize pure and impure in a hierarchical relation- ship on a single continuum. As we have argued earlier, the pure and impure states in which contact is made with the sacred should be treated as qualitatively different. The former is a state in which an individual enters when he is making contact with those sacred cate- gories which do not disturb his cosmization of reality while the latter state marks off those events in which a liminal category (e.g. *preta*) has to be converted into an incorporated category (e.g. ancestor). It is interesting to note that though in the major part of his book on the Coorgs, Srinivas talks of pure and impure as hierarchically arranged he does mention at one stage that these are degrees of *impurity* among the Coorgs but that *madi* or ritual purity is of a different quality altogether (Srinivas, 1952:107).

Finally, it may be pointed out here that an explanation of the variations in the period of birth and death pollution mentioned above must take into account (a) those categories of people who are not affected by pollution, and (b) those categories of people who are doomed to permanent pollution. The former includes the officiating priest who has lit the sacred fires, the king while he is performing the duties of state, an ascetic, a man learned in Vedic lore who has realized the illusory and transitory nature of the world, and a child who has not cut his teeth. Faced with this category, many scholars resort to an explanation either in terms of pragmatism or manipula- tion of rules (see Dumont, 1971). On the contrary, it seems to us that the people who are exempted from these kinds of pollution have one common trait—they stand outside the system. The extreme purity of the officiating priest, while he is in contact with the sacred, separates him from ordinary profane individuals; the king while performing the duties of state is above any social classifications, which alone allows him to judge impartially; the ascetic, as we have

[1] For an interesting application of this model, see Hershman (1974).

already shown, transcends the customary social divisions; the man learned in the Vedas recognizes the illusory (*maya*) character of the social world; and the child has not yet emerged as an incorporated social category. Therefore, if we understand impurity as a metaphor for expressing liminality, the structure of the exemptions becomes clear. We have no need to resort to the kind of explanations that would trace ambiguities in a particular sociological theory to the manipulative tactics of the Brahmans or the pragmatic 'psychology' of the Hindus.

We now come to the category of people who are doomed to permanent impurity, viz. those who are guilty of committing the five great sins (*mahapataka*).[1] It may be argued from this that the punishment for sinners shows the dominance of the ideas of pure and impure. However, as Berger (1969) has shown in a different context, at one level the antonym of the sacred is the profane, defined simply as absence of sacred status. On a deeper level, he argued, the sacred has another opposed category, that of chaos. Since the sacred cosmos emerges out of chaos, man is continuously threatened by the lurking world of chaos, meaninglessness and anomie. Beyond the dangers of punishment by sacred persons lie the more acute dangers of being abandoned by the sacred beings, of losing contact with the sacred and thus being drowned in an abyss of meaninglessness. It is in this context that the punishment for a sinner makes sense. He is doomed to a permanent liminality which in some ways is like that of the ascetic, but only inverse. Whereas the ascetic reaches a state of liminality by a creative transcendence of the ordinary social world, the sinner is reduced to a position of a mere anomaly. His permanent pollution cuts him off from the sacred completely. Not only can he never make contact with the sacred while he lives but even after death he is permanently doomed to lead the existence of a *preta* (ghost). He is not acceptable as a sacrifice to the gods and ancestors, and hence cannot become incorporated as an ancestor. In fact, his cosmic existence as a ghost only repeats his ghost-like existence on this earth. Surely, this mode of punishment to the sinner, the denial of the protection of the sacred against the terrors of chaos, is not unique to Hinduism. The Hindu religious code only uses the idiom of impurity, and those who have been led to believe that the notion of impurity

---

[1] The five great sins are: (1) the murder of a Brahman; (2) drinking intoxicating beverages; (3) sleeping with the wife of a guru; (4) theft; (5) associating with those who have committed these sins.

encompasses the notion of sin have perhaps confused the idiom wi.h the content.

V

We have used the concept of liminality to understand the symbolism of impurity in Hinduism. Liminality may often symbolize a creative transcendence of the given categories of a system. In current anthropological literature there seems to be a much greater concern with understanding the threat of liminality rather than its positive uses. Yet, as early as 1909, Hubert and Mauss emphasized the extraordinary power with which liminality may be imbued. Their essay on Sacrifice (1964) is full of passages which point to the positive uses of ambiguities in social life, as the following passage shows:

This ambiguity is inherent in the very nature of sacrifice. It is dependent, in fact, on the presence of the intermediary and we know that with no intermediary, there is no sacrifice. Because the victim is distinct from the sacrifier and the god, it separates them while uniting them: they draw close to each other, without giving themselves to each other entirely [Hubert & Mauss, 1960: 100].

Thus, it is the ambiguity of sacrifice which makes any contact between the sacred and the profane possible and it is in this that Hubert and Mauss saw the very source of life. In a similar way special powers are bestowed in Hindu belief on the holders of the statuses of Brahman, king and ascetic. These combine in themselves the opposite forces of the profane and the sacred, the social and the cosmic. The Brahman, as Hubert and Mauss argued, stands on the threshold of the sacred and the profane, and represents them at one and the same time. He is referred to as *Bhudevata*, a deity on earth, who links the cosmic and the social. Similarly, the king is said to have a portion of Vishnu in him and the ascetic controls the social and cosmic through his *tapa*. We have described earlier how the very same categories are used to define the conceptual order of Hinduism. The critical importance of the statuses in which the social and cosmic are linked does not lie in the threat which they pose to the distinction of the cosmic and the social or the sacred and the profane but in the manner in which they succeed in ensuring that the social order becomes encompassed in a sacred, cosmic order. If liminality poses dangers these are not only the dangers of darkness but also the dangers of blinding light.

Epilogue

I

IN THIS epilogue, I shall venture outside the monographic structure of my study and attempt to place the conclusions emerging from my analysis in the wider context of discussions on Hinduism. In this way I hope to focus on the basic problematics connected with the mainly anthropological study of Hinduism and elucidate the issues as I see them in the current state of our knowledge. I shall conclude my discussion with some methodological observations on the mode of analysis extensively used in this monograph.

In Chapters 2 and 3, the conceptual structure of Hinduism was abstracted in terms of relations between Brahman, king, and *sanyasi* and we saw how a particular local caste used this conceptual structure to place itself within the Hindu fold. It may now be asked whether the structure abstracted from these texts is common to other texts. We may also ask whether the description of Hinduism in terms of such a synchronic model can be used to interpret and understand diachronic processes in Indian society. The conceptual structure of Hinduism, as we have abstracted it from the caste Puranas of the thirteenth century, describes the totality of terms and relations in Gujarat of the thirteenth century. In no sense does this imply that other ways of defining these terms and relations were not possible but I think it does mean that attempts to arrive at alternative conceptual structures were constrained by the underlying grammar in which the totality of these terms were expected to be used.

In the caste Purana of the Modh Brahmans and Baniyas, we found Brahman, king, and *sanyasi* appear as fully evolved conceptual categories. It is obvious that these terms have a history and carry a heavy semantic load. A proper examination of the history of these terms would involve a study of the Dharmasutra literature, the literature on the Arthashastra, the later Brahmanical codification of sacred laws, and Puranic literature. There are several scholars engaged in this gigantic task and I can only hope to draw on some of these studies for illustrative purposes.

Of the three terms in the conceptual structure of Dharmaranya Purana, let us begin with the king by considering the theories of the origin of kingship. Some scholars of ancient India have pointed out that in some rudimentary form, a theory of elective kingship based upon contract existed in early Brahmanical literature, the earliest hints being found in the Aitareya Brahmana (Drekmeier, 1962: 246). This idea was extensively developed in the Buddhist literature. Tambiah has recently conducted an extensive enquiry into the salient points in which Buddhist conceptions of kingship differed from Brahmanical conceptions (Tambiah, 1976).

Tambiah describes how the Buddhist genesis myth which describes the origin of the world, society, and kingship is marked by two separate movements. The first pertains to forms of existence belonging to this world of sensation (laukika) and the second to the other-world (lokottara) which is the realm of nibbana or release from worldly entanglements. In the first movement, Tambiah says, existence as pure mind is said to slowly degenerate by increasing materiality. Finally, disorder emerges with private property and necessitates the election of a king. Thus, the golden age in such Buddhist sources as the Digha Nikaya is an age in which the ethereal dominated the corporeal. It is only after men become slaves of their passions and such institutions as that of private property emerge that a king has to be appointed to establish order. What is important from our point of view is to observe that it is after the establishment of kingship that the four varnas, as the constitutive units of society, are created and among these four varnas the Kshatriyas are given precedence over the Brahmans.

As many scholars have noted, it is in the Shanti Parva of the Mahabharata that a new theory of the origin of kingship is found. Tambiah feels that by the time the Shanti Parva was written the Buddhist theory of kingship had been absorbed in Brahmanical theories. While it is true that the importance given to kingship in the Shanti Parva may have been in response to Buddhist theory which treats the king as the pivotal agency in the first emergence of societal order (as distinct from the other-worldly order of the monks), the differences and inversions in the Shanti Parva cannot be overlooked.

First of all, kingship is not treated as elective in the Shanti Parva, but is a divine creation. In response to the question posed by Yudhishthira as to why the king, who is no different from other men, governs others, the dying sage Bhishma gives the following explanation. In the first and purest age of the world there was neither kingdom nor king since people followed their code of conduct (*dharma*) voluntarily. Subsequently there was a moral decline in people due to the movement of time. Such terrible disorder emerged that the gods themselves were frightened and approached Vishnu. He expounded the theory of coercive power, and created a son who would rule the people. This son, Virajas, however, determined to follow a life of renunciation as did his two lineal descendants. Finally King Ananga of this lineage agreed to rule but his own son was not given to austerities like his lustrous ancestors. The moral decline in the rulers manifests itself in the evil king Vena who had to be slain by the sages. As we know, from the dead Vena the sages churned out the good king Prithu who ruled in accordance with the advice of Brahmans.

The difference between this story about the origin of kingship and Buddhist theory is obvious. Although both theories reserve the origin of kingship to the age of moral decline, in the Buddhist case the king is said to be elected whereas in the Shanti Parva he is created by god. Moreover, the renunciatory ideal in the Shanti Parva is clear with the first three kings choosing not to rule. Most importantly, the creation of the king *follows* the creation of *varnas* in contrast to the Buddhist case where it precedes the creation of *varnas*. It may also be noted that the good king Prithu rules in accordance with the advice of Brahmans, thus conforming to the theory that kingship derives its legitimacy from the higher domain of the Brahman.

It may be recalled that in the Dharmaranya Purana, it was the Brahman who was treated as the pivotal agency in realizing the cosmic order among men, the emergence of kingship being reserved for a later age. From the story of the origin of kingship in the Shanti Parva, it would seem that in the agreement to rule, there is an implicit departure from the renunciatory ideal, but as the Dharmaranya Purana makes clear, the Brahman too has to depart from this ideal in agreeing to perform priestly functions for the king. Thus the emergence of kingship alters the mutual relationships between the categories of *sanyasi*, king, and Brahman. Incidentally, this also exemplifies the tendency in the texts to propose major conceptual changes by retaining the elements of discourse but changing their relations; or by investing old lexical items with new meanings.

As we suggest, the Dharmaranya Purana presents Brahmans as pursuing renunciatory ideals in the earlier ages and as recipients of gifts and performers of priestly functions for the king in later ages. It is, therefore, interesting to compare the conception of the Brahman in the texts of the earlier period. We shall draw mainly on Heesterman's excellent study (1964) of changing conceptions of the Brahman in pre-classical and classical texts.

Heesterman argues that in the pre-classical sacrificial ritual, Brahmans and Kshatriyas do not seem to form closed groups. Rather, the ritual establishes an alternating pattern in which the *yajamana* passes on the evil of death to the priest, and the Brahman, who at one stage is a recipient of this evil, is encouraged to transfer back this evil to the *yajamana* through gifts and feasts. The role of the Brahman as a recipient of evil undergoes a major transformation in the classical period according to Heesterman, and the Brahman emerges as an incumbent of absolute purity. His position, however, is ambiguous since he is required to safeguard his purity by remaining aloof from the gifts and food of others but is simultaneously in need of a patron in order to exercise his liturgical skills.

Discussing the attitude of the Brahman to the acceptance of gifts, Heesterman says:

Actually brahmanical theory does not and cannot give scope to the gift to the full extent of its meaning. Though it is more than ever meritorious to give, the brahmin has to feel a strong aversion against accepting, as he clearly does. He does not accept the *daksinas* in a direct way but 'turning away' from them and assigning them to various deities. [Heesterman, 1964]

Extensively documenting the Brahman's hesitation in accepting gifts, Heesterman clearly shows that the Brahman as priest is a recipient of negative, inauspicious, evil forces and hence his purity cannot be traced to his priestly functions. He ends by suggesting that the source of the Brahman's purity is not his priestly function with its consequent obligation to accept gifts but his adherence to the values of the renouncer which he brings into the world of the householder. He quotes from the hierarchy of Brahmans developed in Manu, according to the stores of grain they possess. The smaller the store, the higher the Brahman. The ideal of the Brahman, therefore, is one who, while entering into relations with the world, yet remains outside it. We have seen the striking manner in which the Puranic myths show the ideal of the Brahman as pursuing knowledge and resisting the performance of priestly functions. In fact, the tension between these two aspects of the status of the Brahman manifests itself in many ways and we hope that we have been successful in demonstrating that the source of the Brahman's prestige lies in his personification of the renouncer's values. This is what makes him the ideal person to receive gifts although, paradoxically, the very act of acceptance lowers his prestige. It must, surely, be the greatest weakness of Dumont's theory that he fails to notice this particular tension in the definition of a Brahman. I would, therefore, argue along with Heesterman that it is not the Brahman as priest who provides value to the system but the Brahman as a person charged with the duty of following renunciatory ideals. In such a system, the renouncer can hardly be dismissed as being outside the system, for it is he who provides the measure of things. The Brahman as priest is not operating in the domain of purity alone, as Dumont wrongly supposes, but is consistently taking on the inauspicious, evil forces of death from his patron.

The category of *sanyasi* also owes much to Buddhist reflection on renunciatory ideals. In the Buddhist genesis myth, the first movement which corresponds to the emergence of the societal order discussed earlier is followed by a second movement in which monks from all four *varnas* are drawn and organized into monastic orders (Tambiah, 1976). Although the *parivrajaka* tradition of wandering from home into homelessness was very ancient as Dutt (1960) has argued, the wandering sects do not seem to have been organized into monastic orders before the emergence of Buddhism. In fact, Heesterman (1964, 1978) has argued that life in the community and life in the forest constituted two alternating poles in some sacrificial rituals of the Brahmana period. It seems that Buddhism separated these two poles from one another, bringing out a structural hiatus between the societal order (*laukika*) and the other-worldly order (*lokottara*). This corresponds to the opposition between householder and Buddhist monk, which is expressed in early Buddhist literature in a variety of ways. Thus the monk was not allowed to stay in one place for more than three days, except in the rainy season, bringing out the contrast between the stable householder and the homeless wanderer. As Chakravarti (1981) points out, the worst insult to a monk was to call him a shaven householder.

It is interesting to note that the contrast between the householder and the *sanyasi* appears as a central contrast in the Dharmaranya

Purana. Thus it seems that the Hindu *sanyasi* can be seen as parallel to the Buddhist *bhikku*. Yet a search for similarities should not blind us to important relations of inversion. It seems to me that these relations of inversion are to be found in the relation that the Buddhist monk bears to other social categories, such as the householder, the Brahman, and the followers of other sects.

Let us begin with the contrast in the relation between Buddhist monk (*bhikku*) and householder on the one hand, and the relation between *sanyasi* and householder on the other. Although the early Buddhist texts stress the contrast between monk and householder, they also enjoin upon the monk the obligation to collect his food from the householder in the course of the daily alms-round that he is expected to undertake. The Buddhist monk is not encouraged to live off the products of nature. A strict ethic is prescribed according to which he has to accept whatever food has been cooked in the household. He is not allowed to express any preferences nor to accept any money in place of the food. Neither is he allowed to accept an invitation on the exhortation of another monk or nun. In fact, he is expected to stand silently with his begging bowl till the householder offers him food from the hearth. Thus the daily alms-round enjoined upon the monk requires him to enter into a regular relationship with the householder. The rule that monks could accept only cooked food differentiates them from the Brahman, the traditional offering to whom was uncooked food offered by the householder.[1]

The renunciatory ideal followed by the *sanyasi* in the Dharmaranya Purana and in other Puranic texts is one which stresses a complete independence of the *sanyasi* from the world of the householder. He is encouraged either to abstain from food altogether or to eat roots and fruits which grow in the wild. In the matter of dress also, the *sanyasi* remains naked or dresses himself in bark, leaves, or the hide of wild animals. In other words he lives off the produce of nature. It is interesting to observe that even in the matter of dress, the Buddhist monk is earlier enjoined to make his robes from rags collected from garbage and graveyards. Later, when the Buddha is said to have allowed monks to accept new robes from householders, it is on condition that the cloth is cut into small pieces and then these are sewn together so that the monk's robes resemble a 'ploughed field'.

[1] The rules regulating acceptance of food and clothes by the Buddhist monk may be found in the translations of Vinay texts by Horner (1949).

Thus it seems clear that the elaborate rules which ensured a regular relationship between householder and monk served to distinguish the monk from the Hindu *sanyasi*. In fact, one might draw attention to the different types of terms used for the Buddhist monk (*bhikku*) and the renouncer (*sanyasi*), the former referring to begging and non-accumulation and the latter to abandonment. The manner in which these different modes of renunciation may have been later combined in the evolution of this category seems to be an important area for future research.

The differences in the Buddhist mode of renunciation and the wanderer tradition followed by other ascetic sects in the Buddha's time is not only implicit in the rules of conduct but is also positively enunciated in many of the rulings of the Buddha.

On the one hand, monks were not allowed to indulge in any preference regarding the material, texture or shape of their robes. On the other hand, they were also not allowed to appear dishevelled like members of other sects. One of the instances discussed in the Suttavibhanga of Vinaya Pittaka is as follows:

Now at that time, monks thought: 'It is allowed by the lord when staying in lodgings in the jungles to lay aside one of the three robes inside a house.' Those, laying one of the three robes inside a house, were away for more than six nights. These robes were lost and destroyed, and burnt and eaten by the rats. The monks became badly dressed, wearing shabby robes. [Other] monks spoke thus:
    'How is it that your reverences are badly dressed, wearing shabby robes?' [Horner, 1945: 45–6]

This instance shows the chastisement of monks who appeared shabbily dressed. Another instance in the same text explicitly draws the contrast between Buddhist monks and monks of other sects.

Now at that time several monks were travelling along the high road from Saketa to Savatthi. Midway on the road, thieves issuing forth plundered these monks. Then these monks said: 'It is forbidden by the lord to ask a man or woman householder who is not a relation, for a robe.' And being scrupulous, they did not ask, [but] going naked as they were to Savatthi, they saluted the monks respectfully. The monks said:
    'Your reverences, these Naked Ascetics are very good because they respectfully saluted these monks.'
    They said, 'Your reverences, we are not Naked Ascetics, we are monks.'
    Those who were modest monks spread it about, saying, 'How can

monks come naked? Should they not be covered with grass or leaves?' [Horner, 1945: 45–6]

On hearing the instance quoted above, the Buddha is said to have allowed monks to ask for robes in such periods of crisis. He rules that if a monk was unable to obtain any kind of covering, he was to come covered in grass or leaves but not naked like members of other sects.[1]

The passage above shows how the Vinay texts sought to combine the renunciatory ideal enjoined upon the Buddhist monk with an obligation on his part to receive gifts of food and clothes from the householder. Various instances discussed in the Vinay texts also show the concern to distinguish the Buddhist monk from members of other sects. In some senses, one may say that the Buddhist monk may be compared to the Brahman whose obligation to receive gifts is clearly enunciated in the texts of the classical period and is a subject of lively mythical reflection, as the Dharmaranya Purana shows. I think two rules, however, distinguish the monk from the Brahman. First, the monk could accept only cooked food and not uncooked food like the Brahman. Secondly, the monk was not allowed to accept food from the same householder every day, and the rules which asserted his duty to move away from a place after three days must have ensured that a stable gift-receiving relation did not develop between the monk and any particular householder. In contrast, the status of the patron from whom the gift was received was of great importance for the Brahman, as Heesterman (1964) shows; and this is confirmed in the Puranic myths.

It is interesting to note that in the Vinay texts, we find some rules in which the monk and the Brahman are contrasted, and others in which they are treated together. As already stated, the Buddhist monk is exhorted to accept *cooked* food without any discrimination from any devotee while the *smriti* texts try to safeguard the purity of the Brahman by setting out strict rules about the people from whom the Brahman could not accept food. On the other hand, the Vinay texts often lump together the categories Shraman and Brahman, when the renunciatory ideal is being praised in contrast to the this-worldly concern of the householder. The tendency to contrast the Brahman with the renouncer in some contexts and merge him with the latter in other contexts continues till the caste Puranas.

[1] A detailed analysis of these categories in early Buddhist literature can be found in Chakravarti (1981).

We hope that this discussion illustrates the generality of the issues and categories with which we have been dealing within our monographic framework. It seems imperative to us that a concern with history should combine concern with the structural categories of a given society, for the latter are continuously redefined and manipulated in different social contexts.

II

Having discussed some of the variations in the structural interrelations between the categories of Brahman, king, and *sanyasi*, let us now turn to a discussion of the implications of the analysis of domestic rituals and the categories of pure and impure. It was emphasized in Chapter 4 that the categories of right and left, as they appear in domestic rituals, cannot be assimilated in the categories of pure and impure. It seems to us that the separation between these two sets of categories may provide one with a firmer conceptual apparatus within which to view various aspects of Hindu myths and rites. Before we turn to these, however, it may be recalled that impurity (*asaucha*) is seen as both auspicious and inauspicious, pointing to the intersection between these two categorical dimensions. Srinivas's (1952) account of Coorg rituals also shows that auspicious (*mangala*) events could include pure events such as marriage and impure events such as the menstruation of a girl. It is also interesting to note that dictionaries which operate on the principle of classifying associative fields of words on the basis of affinity of meaning, do not resort to an equivalence between words belonging to these two categories. For example, the terms for auspicious—*shubha, mangala, kalyana*—are used with reference to each other; while terms for purity—*shuddha, nirmala, pavitra*—are used as a separate set of equivalences, although this set does not include the specialized *asaucha*, the term for impurity incurred at birth and death. Classical anthropological works on Hinduism, including the influential writings of Srinivas and Dumont, have confounded these categorical distinctions.

Dumont (1978), in a paper on the general subject of ideology recently published by him, has an interesting discussion on the interpretation of lateral symbolism in recent anthropological literature. Deploring the tendency of treating the opposition of right and left as an equi-statutory or symmetrical opposition, he points out that in this case the two poles do not have an equal status. In an elegant formulation, he says that a symmetrical opposition may be reversed at will, whereas the reversal of an asymmetrical opposition always signals the importance of an event, the movement to a different level of life, since the reversed opposition is not the same as the initial opposition. Following this formulation, one may say that the pre-eminence given to the left in death rituals signifies a shift in the level of life.

This formulation marks a welcome shift in Dumont's own approach to the understanding of reversals. He now concedes that in his earlier analysis of a folk deity in Tamilnadu, hierarchy had been approached only indirectly and he had leaned towards the treatment of the right–left opposition as a sole distinctive opposition (Dumont, 1979:811). It is his dismissal of reversals, especially in the context of death rituals, that we had earlier found problematic.[1]

The pre-eminence given to one particular side of the body, whether right or left, however, may itself be expressed in three different ways. At the risk of some repetition I must point out that the opposition of the right and left may be expressed through exclusion, use of spatial juxtaposition, or temporal succession. For example, in some ritual acts the use of one hand is prescribed and the other proscribed while in other cases both hands may be prescribed but one may be placed above or below the other. The use of temporal succession to order the relations between right and left usually orients the body in rela-

---

[1] In the second edition of *Homo Hierarchicus*, Dumont (1980) comments upon the critique of his theory of pure and impure, written by Uberoi and me in 1971. He calls our arguments ingenious and points out the problems involved in returning to the categories of good sacred and bad sacred proposed by us then. He, however, not only fails to take into account my later publication on pure and impure (Das, 1976b), but also disregards the arguments about lateral symbolism proposed by me in 1973 (Das, 1973, 1976b), although my insistence that the opposition of right and left must be considered with reference to the body is very similar to his own later formulation. Uberoi and I have been chastised for not responding to the argument on pure and impure in 1959, when Dumont published his first formulation in a review of Srinivas's study of the Coorgs. A mild protest may be in order here since I was not in the profession in 1959 and in fact had not finished school. However, Uberoi and I had taken serious note of his 1959 paper, as shown by a direct quotation from this in our critique of 1971. In any case I wish the *content* of the arguments could have been considered, especially since my later essays clearly disprove Dumont's somewhat simple idea that our earlier formulation had confused the condition of the corpse with the condition of the mourner.

tion to another object. For example, the rule that in some ritual acts the subject must move from left to right or vice versa. It would be interesting to find out whether these three different modes, i.e. exclusion, simultaneity, and succession, which order the relation between right and left, express differences at the level of the content of ritual acts.

The second major formulation that we had proposed in relation to the right and left was that it represented one particular mode of dividing the body. Thus, it was not only assumed that the opposition of right and left made sense only in relation to a higher totality, that of the body, but also that this particular mode of dividing the body must be seen along with other modes of dividing the body encountered in Hindu thought and ritual. A consideration of both these issues was noticeably absent in Dumont (1970) and later writers such as Brenda Beck (1972), who had concerned themselves with an analysis of the symbols of laterality. Dumont now forcefully makes the point that the right–left opposition makes sense only in relation to the totality of the body, but still seems unconcerned with other modes of dividing it.

A brief recapitulation of the three distinct modes of dividing the body encountered in texts relating to the myth and ritual of the Hindus which were identified in earlier chapters may be useful. The division of the body into the right and left, we argued, uses the idea of mirror opposites—two parts whose asymmetry lies in their inversion. In our own texts, this distinction was encountered in the context of domestic rituals associated with life, and domestic rituals associated with death. In other textual and ethnographic contexts it has been used to classify sects and castes. Secondly, the body may be divided into different parts—e.g. head, arms, trunk, feet—as in the celebrated Parusha Sukta hymn, to refer to the different *varna* categories. In this case each part is conceived as separate and ranked in relation to the totality of the body, although each part is equally necessary to the constitution of the whole. Thirdly, in the context of pure and impure as defined in rites of transition, the body comes to be conceptualized in terms of its centre and peripheries. Play on the symbols of the body may seek to define it as constrained and bounded, or as free-flowing and disarticulated, corresponding to the purity or impurity of the persons participating in a ritual. Now, the major departure in the position taken in this book from the dominant position of Dumont and his followers, is that the latter consider the pure–

impure opposition to be the basic opposition, whereas we contend that these modes of dividing the body correspond to fundamental differences in the conceptualization of the totality. Therefore, relations between *varnas*, between life and death, and between pure and impure are not conceptualized as either homologous or reducible to one another.

Once we have accepted that the pure–impure dichotomy is not the fundamental dichotomy to which all others can be reduced, we should try to see if the intersection of the two axes of auspicious and inauspicious on the one hand and pure and impure on the other can generate a scheme within which domestic and cosmic rituals may be understood.[1] As a rough representation, the following diagram may provide the point of departure, with the warning that the examples taken here are purely for illustration.

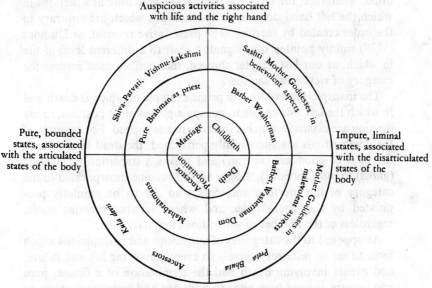

In the diagram above, let us first consider the categories of auspicious and inauspicious. As we have said, auspicious events may be said to be associated with life, and are represented by the right side

---

[1] The distinction between auspiciousness and purity has been used by Marglin (forthcoming) and Madan (1980). Madan makes the interesting suggestion that the scheme of *shubha* (auspiciousness) and *shuddha* (pure) should be related to the scheme of *desh* (place), *kala* (time) and *patra* (person as vessel).

of the body, while inauspicious events may be said to be associated with death, and are represented by the left side of the body. A further formulation, through a consideration of the indigenous categories of right and left now seems possible. The terms in the Sanskrit language for right and left are, respectively, *dakshina* and *vama*. The term *dakshina* shares its root with *daksina* which, along with other meanings, is considered the personification of sacrifice. It is well recognized that sacrifice provides a microcosm for representing the forces of the macrocosm through a symbolic language that seeks to establish *bandhutas*, or relationships between the sacrifice and the universe (Gisbert-Sauch, 1977). In this sense, the *yajna* or sacrifice in the Brahmana provides the principle of order in which events that are started have a future. The word *vama*, which refers to the left hand, also means the contrary, the reversal of the normal order. Therefore, the language itself leads us to look at situations in which the left hand dominates as situations which are contrary to the order created by sacrifice. The prescriptive reversal, as Dumont (1978) rightly pointed out, signals a shift to a different level of life in which, as our last chapter showed, the sacrifice itself merges the category of victim and sacrifier.

The inauspicious events, the prime example of which is death and in which the left side comes to occupy a pre-eminent position, in my opinion are events in which a future is not envisaged. For example, if the death rituals are successfully performed, the dead man follows the path of goodness (*sadgati*) and makes a transition from *preta* (ghost) to *pitr* (ancestor). Slowly he will become incorporated in the category of the fourteen ancestors who are to be regularly propitiated by the householder and whose number remains static, regardless of the number of generations that have died.

As opposed to the categories of auspicious and inauspicious which seem to me to refer respectively to events involving life and future, and events involving death and the termination of a future, pure and impure as used here refer to bounded and articulated states as opposed to liminal and disarticulated states.[1] In the contexts of both auspicious and inauspicious events, we come across persons who are in disarticulated, liminal states. As we have shown, ritual seeks to lead such persons to articulated and bounded states. The use of spatial categories such as thresholds, or places where four roads meet,

---

[1] The use of the terms articulated and disarticulated was suggested to me by McKim Marriott, and I gratefully accept this suggestion.

signals the liminal states whereas the processes of enclosing space signal the bounded ones. Similarly, the body in a free-flowing state with loose hair, unknotted garments, unpared nails, corresponds to the liminal states of a person whereas the bounded states are signalled by the tying of hair, knotting of garments, paring of nails, and use of ornaments.

Before we move to a consideration of the diagrammatic representation given on page 143, it is pertinent to remark that in terms of linguistic categories, *shubha* and *ashubha* are similar to *saucha* and *asaucha* in the sense that the prefix *a* acts as a marker of negation. This similarity of expression corresponds to a similarity of content at one level, since both *ashubha* and *asaucha* are 'marked' states rather than general modes of existence. At another level, however, it seems to me that the well-defined term in the *shubha-ashubha* pair is *shubha*, whereas the primary term in the *saucha-asaucha* pair is *asaucha*. This is because *shubha* is usually defined in positive terms, such as *mangala*, *svasti*, and *ashubha* by the absence of these, while in the *saucha-asaucha* pair the former is defined in terms of an absence of *asaucha*. This is too complex a matter to be mentioned so briefly, but clearly the semantics of these pairs need to be researched by those who have the competence to examine the sources in Sanskrit on these issues.

Now to return to the diagrammatic representation on page 143, the rituals, ritual specialists, and deities are shown as corresponding to one of the four categories generated by the cross-cutting axes of auspicious–inauspicious and pure–impure. It will be seen that marriage is shown as corresponding to the category of pure and auspicious. The characterization of the period of birth as *shubha asaucha*, auspicious impurity, itself gives us a clue to its place in the classificatory schema. Death corresponds to inauspicious impurity, while ancestor propitiation has been placed within the category of inauspicious purity. It must be stressed that although the diagrammatic representation given here is in terms of a static taxonomy, ritual essentially involves a movement from one category to another. For example in the case of death rituals, the living person becomes a *preta* and then is converted into the category of *pitr* or ancestor. Thus the essential movement in death rituals remains within the category of the inauspicious, but from the disarticulated liminal category of *preta* the dead man moves to the well-articulated category of ancestor.

Secondly, it must also be noted that although rituals such as marriage do not involve any impurity, they do invoke ideas of danger. It seems to me that the role of the 'impure' castes such as barber, washerman, etc. in these 'pure' rituals is to protect the subject of rituals from the danger of the evil eye, or danger emanating from such disarticulated cosmic entities as ghosts of various varieties. Inden and Nicholas (1977) describe the sounds made by women to drive away evil forces, at crucial segments of the wedding rituals in Bengal. I have myself observed the recitations of the barber to drive away evil beings at the moment when the bride and the groom first behold each other. Kaushik (1979) and Belliappa (1980) similarly describe the role of the barber and washerman in the wedding rituals of the Doms of Banaras and the Coorgs of south India, respectively. Thus, it is important to note the syntagmatic succession in a ritual, for we may find that the role of these 'impure' castes in 'pure' rituals makes perfect sense if we allow for equal primacy to ideas of auspiciousness, inauspiciousness and danger, along with ideas of pure and impure (cf. Das and Uberoi, 1971).

If we keep the above formulation in mind, we may be able to better understand why some ritual specialists remain in a single category while others fall in more than one category. The ethnographic accounts of rituals of transition show that members of certain castes, such as the Doms, participate only in death rituals and ancestor propitiation. Rather than look at these variations as constituting contradictions to the principle of the separation of pure and impure, as some have done, we should prefer to see this in terms of the nature of the precise events in the rituals in which the participation of these castes is required. As an instance, we may quote Meena Kaushik's (1976) analysis of death rituals, which shows that the barber prepares the corpse, and shaves the head of the mourner at the beginning of cremation. In contrast it is the Dom who deals with the *preta* form that the dead man is supposed to take, and the Mahabrahman who presides over the rituals dealing with the dead man as ancestor. The participation of the barber, Dom, and Mahabrahman in death rituals is not simultaneous but occurs in syntagmatic succession, which in turn corresponds to the movement of the dead man from corpse to *preta*, and finally to ancestor. Similarly, the barber and washerman's participation in marriage rituals may be confined to the role of protecting the subjects of the ritual from malevolent forces in the cosmos and society. Thus, when a ritual specialist appears in more than one category, there may nevertheless be a consistency in their roles if we look at the precise events of the ritual over which they preside. It is also interesting to note that in many events the affines may substitute for members of the servicing castes. I have examined these substitutions in detail elsewhere (Das, 1979), but the point is that far more importance needs to be given to an understanding of the syntagmatic succession in a ritual, if the interaction between notions of auspicious/inauspicious on the one hand, and pure/impure on the other, is to be understood.

Finally, a brief discussion on the classification of deities may be attempted here. This is more in the nature of suggestions for future work rather than a conclusion emerging from a discussion of the previous work. We have seen that as in the case of ritual specialists, cosmic entities might also correspond to a single category, e.g. the inauspicious impure, or spill into more than one category. For example, such cosmic entities as *bhuta*, *preta*, *chudail* are often described as disarticulated entities—often forms of a dead person whose transformation to the category of ancestor could not be completed. As discussed in the last two chapters, they are often confined to cremation grounds, roaming around in darkness and the only rituals addressed to them are rituals of exorcism. In contrast, mother goddesses fall in various categories—some preside over childbirth as the goddess Sashti in Bengal, others can bring disease and death, and still others are worshipped along with ancestors. It seems to me that the mythology of these goddesses show their oscillation between these categories (cf. Wadley, 1980; Kaushik, 1979; Belliappa, 1980). The story of the goddess Ankalamman, quoted from the study of Beck (1972) in Chapter 4, may be recalled here. From a sorceress of the burning grounds, she succeeded in getting herself installed as the *kula devi*, the lineage goddess, of a powerful patron. Similarly Wadley (1980) has described how Shitala may be worshipped as both the goddess of disease and the goddess who ensures the welfare of children. Just as subjects of rituals may move from one category to another, so the mythology of the gods and goddesses provide a clue to their movement between these categories.

In the first instance, it may seem that the gods of the great tradition are not subject to these movements. However, it is important to remember that the gods described in the Sanskrit texts have many forms, and different names to signal the particular form in which the deity is being worshipped. For example, although both Durga and

Kali are said to be different forms of Parvati, their modes of propitiation are different. At this juncture, it is important to recall that in her form as Parvati, the goddess is incapable of meeting the threat from demons.[1] Only in her Durga or Kali form can she meet such a threat. So it seems that just as one gets the reversal of the normal use of right and left hands during such periods as death and ancestor propitiation, signalling the move to a new level of life, so does one get a reversal of the normal hierarchy of gods and goddesses during periods of cosmic disturbances, with male gods being dependent upon goddesses, and further the disarticulated forms of the goddess taking precedence over her articulated and bounded forms.

I hope the preceding discussion has succeeded in pointing out the new categories for exploration, both through textual analysis and fieldwork. There is one last point about pure and impure which should be mentioned here. In the last chapter I suggested that there may be many kinds of impurity, and expressed my discomfort at identifying these as constituting a single type. In fact, the existence of many lexical items to express different kinds of impurity points to the need for examining these separately in the first instance. For example, *asaucha* refers strictly to the impurity incurred on birth and death and is separate from such terms as *jutha* (contaminated), *ashuddha* (sullied), *achhuta* (not to be touched). As Chapter 4 tried to show, the relations between castes in everyday contexts are governed by notions of separation and ranking. For example, the same Dom from whom the most exclusive Brahman has to accept fire for cremating a dead body, remains an untouchable to him in everyday life. It is not to the conjunction of roles and positions of the so-called impure castes in sacred and secular contexts, but to the disjunction in their position in everyday life and in the circumscribed contexts of rituals of various kinds, that we should like to draw attention here.

We now come to the crucial issue of seeing how the categorical division between Brahman, king, and *sanyasi* relates to the two cross-cutting axes of auspicious/inauspicious and pure/impure discussed above. The first point to note is that the categories Brahman, king, and *sanyasi* have a dual aspect, so to say: one relating to their life-giving and life-preserving aspects and the second relating to the darker, inauspicious events associated with death. The Brahman, as pure priest, may preside over such auspicious events as rites of

---

[1] This theme is clearly found in the mythology of the goddess (cf. Shankarayanan, 1968).

pregnancy, marriage, entry into a new house, etc. In the case of inauspicious events imbued with danger, it is only Brahmans of a low status who would agree to act as ritual specialists. In the myths of origin of such castes as Doms and Mahabrahmans, who preside over death rituals, their status as fallen Brahmans is emphasized. The fall is usually attributed to the necessity on the part of some ancestor to accept food or gifts on the occasion of ancestor propitiation or death. In Sanskrit the term Mahabrahman means a Brahman devoid of all learning, the word *maha* (great) being used ironically. Thus, the nature of the event in which Doms and Mahabrahmans participate imbues them with the darkness of death, but their roles are nevertheless seen as performed by people belonging to the Brahman category. It seems clear, therefore, that one source of variation in the status of groups that define themselves as Brahman is the nature of the event on which they perform their ritual functions. Above these Brahmans who have to appear as the recipients of gifts repeatedly, are placed those Brahmans who have received grants, such as land, from powerful persons, such as kings, once for all, and who can then permanently abstain from receiving gifts from patrons of a lower order.

In the Purana that we analysed, the intimate connection between the Hindu king and the tribal king was suggested in the story of King Vena. To recall, the evil contained in the person of the Hindu king Vena was churned out by the sages, and thus from his left side emerged the ferocious tribal chief to whom the kingdom of the hills was granted. Thus kingship itself seems to be defined in terms of a dual definition, the benevolent, nurturing aspect being coupled with the malevolent and ferocious aspect. Their separation in this myth is achieved by a separation between the tribal king and the Hindu king. In other stories the dual aspects of kingship may be posited in twins, or brothers. The use of lateral symbolism in identifying these two aspects of kingship is clear in the story of King Vena and needs to be researched in greater detail.

A similar duality in the definition of the *sanyasi* is often made in terms of the right hand and left hand division of sects. We had shown how the two modes of transcendence of normal categorical oppositions appear in the text. Members of the right hand sects practise their austerities by abandoning the values of the householder while members of the left-hand sects demonstrate their transcendence by inverting these values. The association of the former with proper performance of sacrifice in his hermitage, and the protection of the proper order of things, is often reiterated in Sanskrit literature, while the association of left-handed sects (*vamapanthi*) with death, cremation grounds, corpses, is well known. Without going into every qualification and providing textual support for every argument made here, I merely wish to draw attention to the fact that the *sanyasi* is capable of inspiring contradictory attitudes such as reverence and fear, depending upon the interpretation placed on his mode of renunciation and asceticism.

It would be obvious that to attribute fixed meanings to the categories of Brahman, king, and *sanyasi* is to misinterpret the whole spirit of this exercise. Rather, one has to examine the semantic field in which a term appears and also to appreciate that the very contradictions in each term give it a dynamism of its own. For example, the Brahman as expressing ideals of renunciation, as a receiver of gifts and as a specialist in funeral rites—these are all shown to be meanings contained in the category Brahman, which are given expression in different local and historical contexts. The point to remember is that for every single meaning of the categorical term that is brought to the surface, there is a class of unexpressed meanings that form a kind of hidden treasure. In Sanskrit poetics it was believed that every word had its own powers, and my analysis of these categories has persuaded me that words can be thought of as pulsating with life, and with a dynamism that comes from the totality of meanings that they can be made to evoke.

III

The last section is devoted to a few methodological issues that need to be stated at this juncture. The adoption of structuralist methods for understanding narrative structures has been rightly accused of overstating the importance of the paradigmatic axis to the neglect of the syntagmatic axis. Yet it is clear that the form of the narrative, at the level of both expression and content, depends upon the correct application of rules of syntagmatic and paradigmatic operations. It is also well known that analytical activity corresponding to the syntagmatic axis of narrative is the activity of carving out while analytical activity corresponding to the paradigmatic field is classification. The actual application of these rules has depended on whether it is a narrative or ritual complex that is being studied (cf. Barthes, 1967).

In our understanding of the Dharmaranya Purana, the syntagmatic operations hold as much importance as the paradigmatic operations. It is clear that the first significant paradigmatic unit that we have carved out from the syntagmatic succession of stories includes the following elements: (i) the creation of Brahmans for the consecration of social space, (ii) the creation of householders, (iii) the Brahman's relation to the *sanyasi*, (iv) the appearance of the king and the re-definition of Brahmans as recipients of gifts in exchange for the performance of sacrifice on behalf of the king; and finally, the negation of the categorical relations established above through the medium of heterodox sects and hence the definition of heterodoxy. To an extent, the unit which is carved out as a significant one from a continuous syntagmatic chain depends upon the judgement of the analyst. Not only does the text continue with more stories which have been seen here as constitutive of a second paradigmatic unit but also this Purana may itself be seen as part of a chain including other versions of the Dharmaranya Purana, and indeed, other Puranas. From this endless text, how does one justify the decision to carve out the set of stories that have been isolated as forming a significant paradigmatic unit? As has been pointed out earlier, the isolation of the significant unit does depend to a large extent on the judgement of the analyst, but this is not a judgement which is formed on criteria that cannot be communicated. In retrospect, it seems to me that within the significant unit isolated by me, the criterion of cumulative accretion provided an important clue. In other words, within this unit the precise order of succession of the stories was important, and could not be ignored for building up the paradigmatic structure. For example, it is of some relevance to us that the Purana does not begin with the creation of a king as the first social category but with the creation of Brahmans. Similarly, the role of Brahmans as gift-recipients appears later, as we have shown, and this is of importance in our understanding of the inner contradictions in the definition of a Brahman. Furthermore, it is after the myths establish the relations between Brahman, king and *sanyasi* that a definition of heterodox sects emerges. In fact, the syntagmatic sequence was an important tool in the hands of writers who could often convey their differences by re-arranging the sequence in which categories, myths, or ritual events occurred. To take a simple example, the four *varnas* are enumerated in Buddhist literature but the order of enumeration is altered and Kshatriyas are placed before Brahmans. This simple device signals the greater importance attached to the Kshatriya *varna* in Buddhist literature. Our decision to treat the stories up to the point of rejection and reinstatement of Brahmans by the king under Buddhist influence as forming a significant paradigmatic unit was on the basis that the myths till this point presented a cumulative structure, in which the relative relations between different categories could not be understood without due regard to the order of succession. The establishment of all the categories necessary for the universe of discourse is signalled by the stories about the rejection of these categorical relations.

After the establishment of the first significant unit, carved out from the syntagmatic chain, we move to a new level in the Purana, in which the differences within a caste, in this case the Modh Brahmans and Baniyas, are explained with reference to the tripartite structure established earlier. The relations between the *jatis* are reformulated in terms of the exchange of food, women, and services, in view of the decline of Hindu kingship. Thus local and temporal concerns of a *jati* are, nevertheless, sought to be discussed and understood within the categories established as valid for Hindu civilization. The following representation may make the interplay between syntagmatic and paradigmatic axes somewhat clearer.

The second part of the book dealt with texts relating to the performance of domestic rituals on the one hand, and death rituals on the other. In some senses one may say that the carving out operation is simpler in this case, since ritual acts appear as discrete units. This was the assumption underlying Srinivas's (1952) analysis of the ritual idiom of the Coorgs. Yet, it may be somewhat hasty to assume that a single ritual act provides the significant unit for setting up a system of paradigmatic oppositions. Rather, we have tried to show that it may be more meaningful to compare significant syntagmatic *sequences*, at the level of both myth and rite. For example, in the context of the use of lateral symbolism, a ritual complex may be compared with another not only in the exclusion or inclusion, for instance, of a particular hand but also in terms of the movement from one side to another. A very good example of the importance of the syntagmatic sequence in marriage rituals is found in Inden and Nicholas (1977) and in the culinary code in marriage and death rituals in Belliappa and Kaushik (1980). These studies establish the importance of analysing rituals simultaneously within both the syntagmatic and paradigmatic axes. In my opinion this is an

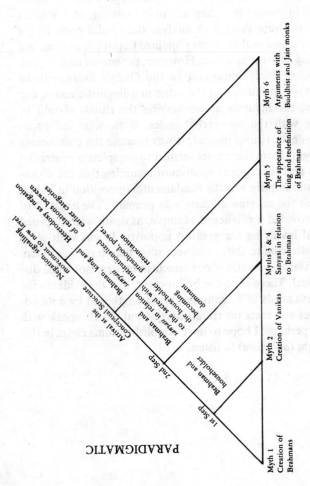

PARADIGMATIC

SYNTAGMATIC

Myth 1
Creation of
Brahmans

Myth 2
Creation of Vanikas

Myths 3 & 4
Sanyasi in relation
to Brahman

Myth 5
The appearance of
king and redefinition
of Brahman

Myth 6
Arguments with
Buddhist and Jain monks

1st Step

2nd Step

Brahman and
householder

Brahman and
vanika in relation
to the sacred with
the householder
becoming
dominant

Brahman, king and
sanyasi
Institutionalized
priesthood, power,
renunciation

Arrival at the
Conceptual structure

Heterodoxy as negation
of relations between
earlier categories

Negation, signalling
movement to new level

Note: The diagram above shows how each step on the paradigmatic axis is built up till we arrive at the relations between Brahman, king, and *sanyasi*. Till this point, syntagmatic succession is of great importance in arriving at the structure of the terms. After this, the relations between Brahman, king, and *sanyasi* are treated as fully evolved and in the discussion on *jatis* within the Modh Brahmans, the syntagmatic succession of the first six myths is ignored, and only the final relations between the categories of Brahman, king, and *sanyasi* are considered. This is an illustration of the logic that we have been discussing.

important corrective to the tendency in structuralist interpretations of myth and ritual to emphasize system at the cost of event, and the paradigmatic at the cost of the syntagmatic.

Our concluding with a reference to a hiatus in the two parts of this book is an obvious indication that the monographic method could not be followed in the last two chapters. In our analysis of Gobhila's Grihya Sutra, we were careful to analyse the spatial code in the entirety of the text and to that extent remained faithful to our method of understanding the text as a unit. However, the spatial code, which appears to be extremely important in the Grihya Sutra, can be further understood in relation to the other non-linguistic codes, e.g. colour. Finally, the *mantras* accompanying the rituals should be analysed along with the non-verbal codes. If we were led to an analysis of the death rituals instead, it was because the conclusions that were emerging from these texts seemed to completely contradict the established anthropological wisdom of assuming that the dichotomy of pure and impure was the fundamental opposition in Hindu society and that the religion of caste was primary. The analysis of death rituals provided a privileged example, as death was supposed to be the ritual involving the greatest impurity. It was with some regret that the decision to shift to issues rather than texts was taken. It seemed necessary to do this if our conclusions were not to be dismissed as atypical. There is no doubt, however, that the evidence for these conclusions needs to be considerably strengthened by a monographic study of the texts on ritual. Myths and rituals speak with many tongues, perhaps. I hope to have established some claim in this study to the right (*adhikara*) to listen.

Appendix 1

achhūta	dharma	Kalikā
adhikāra	dharma-kūpa	Kaliyuga
ādipuruṣa	Dharmarāja	Kalivarjya
Agni	Dharmāraṇya	kalpānta
āgya	Dharmaśāstra	kalyāṇa
Āma	Dhaumya	kāma
Anāvila Purāṇa	Dhanuja	kāmadhenu
antyeṣṭi saṃskāra	durgati	Kaṇḍola
anuloma	dūrva	Kanyākubja
aśauca	Dvāpara	karma
āśrama		karmakāṇḍa
asura	ekavakyatva	Kaśyapa
aṭṭārikā		Kṛtayuga
	gārhasthya	Kṛtyakalpataru
bālabrahmacārin	Garuḍa Purāṇa	kṣapaṇaka
bali	Gāyatrī	Kṣatriya
bandhutā	Gobhuja	kula
Bauddha	golaka	kuladevī
Bhadrikā	gotra	kumbhīdhānya
Bhaṭṭa Śri Lakṣmīdhara	gṛihastha	Kuṇapa
bhikṣu	Gṛihya Sūtra	kuṇḍa
bhikṣuka		kūpa
bhoga	Hanumat	kuśa
bhogī	Hari	
bhūta	Hariścandra	Lakṣmī
Brahmā	havi	laukika
brahmacarya	Hiraṇyakaśipu	lokottara
Brahmakṣetra	homa	
Brahmakuṇḍa		Māgha
Brahmavarta	Indra	Mahālakṣmī
		mahāpātaka
Cāmara	Jaina	Mahāpurāṇa
Caturvedin	jananāśauca	mahātman
Chattrā	japa	Maheśa
	jāti	Māndhātā
dakṣiṇā	jaya	maṅgala
dāna	Jayadeva	mantra
Daśaratha	Jeṭhimalla	Manu
deśa		maraṇāśauca
Devāṅga Purāṇa	kāla	Māruta
devī	Kalidharmavarṇana	mātā

Mātaṅgī
māyā
mleccha
Mūlarāja
muni

Nāgarakhaṇḍa
namaskāra mantra
nandī
nāndīmukha
nidrā
Nimbajā
nirmala
niyoga

Oṃkāra

Padmapurāṇa
pākhaṇḍī
Palāśa
pañcaka
paṅkti
Paramāraṇḍā
Paraśurāma
Pārvatī
parivrajaka
pātra
pavitrā
piṇḍa
pippala
pitṛ
prācināvītin
pravara
Prayāga
prāyaścitta
preta
pūjā
Purāṇa
Purusa sukta

rājanīti
rājya
Rākṣasa

Rāma
Rāmacandra
Ratnagarigā
Rāvaṇa
ṛṣi
Rudra

Sadgati
Śakti
Śaṃkara
Saṃnyāsa
Saṃnyāsin
sapiṇḍīkaraṇa
Sarasvatī
Śāstra
śikhā
śilocha
Sītā
Śiva
Śivaliṅga
smṛti
śrāddha
śrautakarma
śrautasūtra
Śrīmātā
Śristhala Mahātmya
śubha
śuddhi
Śuddhikāṇḍa
śūdra
Sukhavāsapura
Sūryavaṃśa
sūta
sūtaka
sūtikā
sūtikāṣaṣṭhī
sūtra
Sūtradhāra
sūtri
svasti

tantra
tapa

tapasyā
tīrtha
tīrthāṅkara
Tretā
Trivedī
Triveṇī
Tulasī

Upapurāṇa
Urvaśī

vāma
vāmapanthī
Vaisṇavī
vaiśya
Vālakhilya
vāmapanthī
vaṃśa
vānaprastha
vāṇijya
Vaṇika
varṇa
varṇa-samkara
Vaśiṣṭha
vāstupūjā
Veda
Veṇa
Viṣṇu
Viśvedevāḥ
Viśvakarman
Viśvavasu Gandharva
vrata
vṛtti

yajamāna
yajña
yajñopavītin
Yama
yati
yoga
Yudhiṣṭhira
yuga
yūpa

Appendix 2

A brief introduction to mythological places and persons that appear in the text, primarily based on Dowson's *A Classical Dictionary of Hindu Mythology* (1968) and Sarkar's *Puranic Abhidhan* (in Bengali, 1958).

AAMA   A king not mentioned in any of the dictionaries of Hindu mythology.

ADITI   The daughter of Brahma, wife of Kashyap, and mother of the gods.

BRAHMA   The first member of the Hindu triad. He is the creator of the universe and also the 'first-created'. Is usually represented as having four arms and four faces. He is also known as Prajapati, the lord and father of all creatures.

CHAMATKARA   A king not mentioned in either of the texts.

CHAMUNDA   An emanation of the goddess Durga, sent forth from her forehead to encounter the demons Chanda and Munda.

DHARMARAJA   1. Yama, king of the dead. 2. A title of Yudhishthira who was mythologically a son of Yama.

DHARMARANYA   A holy forest, named after Dharmaraja, in which he performed penance.

DHARMASHASTRAS   A law-book or code of laws. This term includes the whole body of Hindu law, but it is more especially applicable to the laws of Manu, Yajnavalkya and other sages who first recorded the Smriti or 'recollections' of what they had received from a divine source.

DHAUMYA   The family priest of the Pandavas.

DHENUJA   The word literally means born from the cow. It is not mentioned in the two texts on which this Appendix is based.

DWAPARYUGA   The third age of the world, extending to 864,000 years.

GANGA   The sacred river Ganges. The Viyadganga, or heavenly Ganges flows from the toe of Vishnu and was brought down to the earth by the prayers of the saint-king Bhagirath.

GAYATRI   A most sacred verse of the Rigveda, which it is the duty of every Brahman to repeat in his mind during his morning and evening devotions.

GOKARNA   A place of pilgrimage, sacred to Shiva.

HANUMANA   A celebrated monkey-chief. He was the son of Vayu, the Wind god, and Anjani (Anjana). He is a conspicuous figure in the Ramayana. He assisted Rama in his war against Ravana.

HARI   A name of Vishnu, though it is sometimes used for other gods also.

INDRA   The chief of gods. In the Rigveda Indra stood in first rank but in the Puranas he is subordinate to the triad, Brahma, Vishnu, and Shiva.

KALIYUGA   The fourth or present age of the world, which is to endure for 432,000 years.

KAMADHENU   A celestial cow which grants all desires. She belongs to the sage Vashishtha. She is also called Kamaduha, Savala and Surabhi.

KHARANANA A goddess who also finds no mention in the two texts.

KRITAYUGA The first age of the world, a period of 1,725,000 years.

LAKSHMI The goddess of wealth, wife of Vishnu and the mother of Kama (Cupid). She arose from the ocean when it was churned by the gods and demons.

MARUTS The Wind gods who were born from Diti's womb after Indra had divided her unborn child into forty-nine children.

OMKAR The sacred sound 'Om', which can be used in invocation, affirmation, benediction and consent. It is used at the commencement of prayers and religious books.

PARAMARANDA A goddess who is not mentioned in the two texts.

PARASHURAMA The word literally means 'Rama with the axe'. He is considered to be the sixth incarnation of Vishnu. His hostility to the Kshatriyas is well known and is supposed to have originated in the following incident: Once a Kshatriya king called Kritavirya, who had a thousand arms, visited the hermitage of Jamadagni, Parashurama's father. Since Jamadagni was not there, he was entertained by his wife. But when he departed, the king carried off a sacrificial calf. This enraged Parashurama, so much that he cut off Kritavirya's thousand arms and killed him. In retaliation, the sons of Kritavirya killed Jamadagni and for that Parashurama vowed vengeance against the entire Kshatriya race. He is said to have rid the earth of Kshatriyas twenty-one times and given it to the Brahmans.

SARASVATI 1. The goddess of speech and learning. 2. A sacred river which is supposed to have been dried up by the curse of a sage.

SHANKAR A name of Shiva in his creative character.

SHANKARACHARYA The great religious reformer and teacher of Vedanta philosophy, who lived in the eighth or ninth century.

SHIVA The third deity of the Hindu triad, and is represented as the destroying principle. However, his attributes and powers are more numerous. As Rudra, he is the god of destruction. As Shankar, he is 'auspicious' and is the reproductive power which is always restoring or recreating that which has been destroyed. His character as restorer is represented by the *linga* or phallus, which is worshipped. Thirdly, he is the Mahayogi or the great ascetic who represents the highest perfection of meditation and penance. He is also Bhuteshwara, the lord of ghosts and goblins. Besides these major forms in which he is represented, Shiva also has other names and attributes which refer to various legends connected with him.

SITA The daughter of King Janak of Videha who was adopted by him after she had been born from the earth, and the wife of Rama. She accompanied Rama in his exile, but was abducted by Ravana. who used various stratagems to persuade her to become his wife but she remained faithful to Rama. After the battle between Ravana and Rama in which Ravana was killed, she was freed and taken back by Rama. However, since she had stayed in Ravana's palace, some people of Rama's kingdom suspected her innocence and Rama banished her though she was pregnant. She went away to the hermitage of Valmiki. There she gave birth to twin sons. After many years Rama, after having recognized his sons in an encounter, wanted to take Sita back. However Sita, who was deeply wounded, asked the earth to take her back as a proof of her innocence. The ground opened and she returned to the earth from which she had been born.

SURABHI   A name of Kamadhenu.

SUTA   Literally, a charioteer. The Puranas are usually written in the form of a dialogue between Suta and a group of ascetics. Since the stories are recited by the Suta in the Puranas, it is thought that Suta refers to people belonging to mythographer castes.

TRETAYUGA   The second age of the world, a period of 1,296,000 years.

TRIMURTI   The Hindu triad, consisting of the gods Brahma, Vishnu and Mahesh (Shiva). Brahma is the creator of the world, Vishnu the preserver and Shiva the destroyer.

TRIVENI   The place where the sacred rivers Ganga, Yamuna, and Sarasvati meet and flow as a single stream.

URVASHI   A very beautiful dancer in Indra's court. She is very often employed by Indra to seduce ascetics who are engaged in penance so that they will not be able to usurp Indra's throne by the power of their penance.

VASHISHTHA   The family priest of the house of Ikshwaku, to which Rama belonged.

VAYU   A name of Marut, the Wind god.

VISHVADEVAS   All the gods.

VISHNU   The second god of the Hindu triad. He is the preserver of the world. His protective power is manifested in the avatars or 'incarnations' in which a portion of his divine essence was embodied in animal or human form, in order to combat some great evil.

VISHVAKARMAN   The celestial architect who is represented in the Ramayana as having built the city of Lanka for Ravana. In the Puranas, he is the son of Prabhasa and his daughter is married to Surya (Sun).

VISHVAMITRA   A celebrated sage who was born a Kshatriya, but by intense austerities raised himself to the status of a Brahman and became one of the seven great Rishis.

VISHVAVASU GANDHARVA   A chief of the Gandharvas in Indra's heaven; presiding deity of procreation.

VYASA   'An arranger'. The title is common to many old authors and compilers but is specifically applied to the compiler of the Vedas, and the Mahabharata.

YUDHISHTHIRA   The eldest of the Pandavas who were the five sons of Pandu. The battle between the Pandavas and the Kauravas forms the subject-matter of the Mahabharata epic.

References

Bailey, F. G.
 1964 'Two Villages in Orissa (India)', in *Closed Systems and Open Minds*, ed. Max Gluckman. London: Aldine, 52–82.

Barnes, J. A.
 1971 'Time Flies Like an Arrow', *Man*, n.s. 6, 537–52.

Barthes, Ronald
 1967 *Elements of Semiology*, trans. Annette Lavers and Colin Smith. Jonathan Cape Ltd.

Beck, Brenda
 1972 *Peasant Society in Konku: A Study of Right and Left Subcastes in South India*. Vancouver: University of British Columbia.
 1976 'The Symbolic Merger of Body, Space and Cosmos in Hindu Tamilnad', *Contributions to Indian Sociology*, n.s. 10, 213–44.

Belliappa, Jayanthi
 1980 *A Sociological Study of Religious Concepts of the Coorgs*. Unpublished Ph.D. dissertation, University of Delhi.

Belliappa, Jayanthi, and Meena Kaushik
 1980 'The Food of Well-Being'. Paper presented to the Conference on South Asian Political Economy held in New Delhi, 19–21 December.

Berger, Peter
 1969 *The Social Reality of Religion*. Harmondsworth: Penguin.

Boudon, Raymond
 1972 *The Uses of Structuralism*. London: Heinemann.

Carter, Anthony
 1975 'Caste Boundaries, and the Principle of Kinship Amity', *Contributions to Indian Sociology*, n.s. 9, 123–37.

Chakravarti, Uma
 1981 *Social Dimensions of Early Buddhism*. Unpublished Ph.D. dissertation, University of Delhi.

Chakravarty, S.
 1965 'Bangadeshiya Pauranic Parampara', *Purana* (in Sanskrit), Varanasi: Kashiraj Trust.

Das, Veena
 1968 'A Sociological Approach to the Caste Puranas of Gujarat: A Case Study', *Sociological Bulletin*, 17, 141–64.
 1970 'A Sociological Investigation of the Caste Puranas of Gujarat'. Unpublished Ph.D. dissertation, University of Delhi.
 1973 'On the Categorization of Space in Hindu Ritual'. Paper presented to the session on 'The Anthropology of Literary and Oral Sources' convened at the ASA Conference on New Directions in Social Anthropology, Oxford; later published in *Text and Context: The*

Social Anthropology of Tradition (ed. R. K. Jain), Philadelphia: ISHI, 1977.

1976a 'Masks and Faces: An Essay on Punjabi Kinship', *Contributions to Indian Sociology*, n.s. 10, 1–30.

1976b 'The Uses of Liminality: Society and Cosmos in Hinduism', *Contributions to Indian Sociology*, n.s. 10, 245–65.

1978 'Marriage in India: An Approach to the Study of Variation'. Paper presented at the XI International Congress of Anthropological and Ethnological Sciences, New Delhi.

Das, Veena & J. P. S. Uberoi

1971 'The Elementary Structure of Caste', *Contributions to Indian Sociology*, n.s. 5, 33–43.

Dave, K. S.

1962 'Gujaratno, Jnatipurano ane Teerthamahatmya', *Swadhyaya*, Oriental Institute of Baroda.

de Bary, William, *et al.* (comps.)

1958 *Sources of Indian Tradition*. Delhi: Motilal Banarsidas.

Douglas, Mary

1966 *Purity and Danger*. London: Routledge & Kegan Paul.

Dowson, John

1968 *Classical Dictionary of Hindu Mythology and Religion, Geography, History, and Literature*. London: Routledge & Kegan Paul.

Drekmeier, Charles

1962 *Kingship and Community in Early India*. Stanford University Press, California.

Dumézil, Georges

1958 'Métiers et Classes Fonctionnelles Chez Divers Peuples Indo-Européen', *Annales Economies, Sociétés, Civilisations*, 13, 716–24.

Dumont, Louis

1957 'For a Sociology of India', *Contributions to Indian Sociology*, 1, 7–22.

1960 'World Renunciation in Indian Religions', *Contributions to Indian Sociology*, 4, 33–62.

1962 'The Conception of Kinship in Ancient India', *Contributions to Indian Sociology*, 6, 48–77.

1970a *Homo Hierarchicus: The Caste System and Its Implications*. London: Weidenfield & Nicholson.

1970b 'A Structural Definition of a Folk Deity', in *Religion, Politics and History in India*. The Hague: Mouton & Co., 20–32.

1971 'On Putative Hierarchy and Some Allergies to It', *Contributions to Indian Sociology*, n.s. 5, 58–78.

1978 'La communauté anthropologique et l'idéologie', *L'Homme*, 18, 83–110 (English translation in *Social Science Information*, 18 (1979), 785–817).

1980 *Homo Hierarchicus: The Caste System and Its Implications*, 2nd ed., trans. Mark Sainsburg, Louis Dumont, and Basia Gulati. Chicago: University of Chicago Press.

Dumont, Louis & David Pocock

1959 'Pure and Impure', *Contributions to Indian Sociology*, 3, 9–39.

Durkheim, Émile
  1964   *The Elementary Forms of the Religious Life*, trans. Joseph Ward
          Swain. London: Allen & Unwin (first published in 1912).
Dutt, S.
  1960   *Early Buddhist Monachism*. Bombay.
Gerth, H. H. & C. W. Mills
  1948   *From Max Weber: Essays in Sociology*. London: Routledge &
          Kegan Paul.
Ghurye, Govind S.
  1953   *Indian Sadhus*. Bombay: Popular Book Depot.
  1962   *Gods and Men*. Bombay: Popular Book Depot.
Gisbert Sauch, G.
  1977   *Bliss in the Upanishads*. Delhi: Orient Publishers and Distributors.
Heesterman, J. C.
  1964   'Brahman, Ritual and Renouncer', Weiner Zeitschrift fur die
          Kunde Sud-und Ust Asiens, 8, 1–31.
  1978   'Veda and Dharma', in *The Concept of Duty in South Asia*, ed.
          W. D. O'Flaherty and J. Duncan Derett. Delhi: Vikas Publishing
          House.
Herschman, Paul
  1974   'Hair, Sex, and Dirt', *Man*, 9, 274–98.
Hertz, Robert
  1960   *Death and the Right Hand*, trans. Claudia & Rodney Needham.
          London: Cohen & West (first published in 1907 in French).
Hocart, A. M.
  1969   *Kingship*. Oxford: OUP (first published in 1927).
Horner, I. B.
  1949   *The Book of Discipline*, trans. of *Vinaya Pittaka*, vol. III. London:
          OUP.
Hsu, Francis L. K.
  1964   *Clan, Caste, and Club*. Berkeley: University of California Press.
Hubert, H. & M. Mauss
  1964   *Sacrifice: Its Nature and Function*. London: Cohen & West.
Inden, R. B. and R. W. Nicholas
  1977   *Kinship in Bengali Culture*. Chicago: University of Chicago
          Press.
Kane, P. V.
  1941   *History of Dharmashastra*, vol. 2, pt 2. Poona: Bhandarkar Oriental
          Research Institute.
Kapadia, K. M.
  1947   *Hindu Kinship*. Bombay: Popular Book Depot.
Karve, Irawati,
  1953   *Kinship Organisation in India*. Poona: Deccan College.
Kaushik, Meena
  1976   'The Symbolic Representation of Death', *Contributions to Indian
          Sociology*, n.s. 10, 265–92.
  1979   *Religion and Social Structure among the Doms of Banaras*. Un-
          published Ph.D. dissertation, University of Delhi.

Kavi, Dalpatram
  1887   *Jnatinibandha* (in Gujarati). Gujarat: Gujarat Vernacular Society.
Kesavan, V.
  1974a   'Aryan Brahman Settlements of Ancient Kerala.' Unpublished
          M.A. thesis, University of Calicut.
  1974b   'Community Organization and Village Administration in the
          Brahman Settlements of Kerala in the Later Cera Period, *c.* A.D.
          800–1100.' Paper presented to the Indian History Congress at
          Jadavpur University, Calcutta.
Leach, Edmund
  1964   'Anthropological Aspects of Language: Animal Categories and
          Verbal Abuse', in *New Directions in the Study of Language*, ed.
          E. H. Lenneberg. Boston: M.I.T. Press, 23–63.
  1968   'Introduction', *Dialectic in Practical Religion*. Cambridge: Cam-
          bridge University Press, 1–6.
Lévi-Strauss, Claude
  1962   *Totemism.* Harmondsworth: Penguin.
  1963a   'The Bear and the Barber', *Journal of the Royal Anthropological
          Institute*, 93, 1–11.
  1963b   'The Structural Study of Myth', *Structural Anthropology*. New
          York: Basic Books, 206–31.
  1964   *Mythologiques: Le Cru et le Cuit.* Paris: Plon.
  1966   *The Savage Mind.* Chicago: University of Chicago Press.
  1968   'The Story of Asdiwal' (trans. Nicholas Mann), in *The Structural
          Study of Myth and Totemism*, ed. E. Leach. London: Tavistock,
          1–47.
Lingat, Robert
  1962   'Time and Dharma', *Contributions to Indian Sociology*, 6, 7–16.
Macdonell, Arthur A.
  1899   *A History of Sanskrit Literature.* London: William Heinemann.
Madan, T. N.
  1980   '*Shubha* and *Shuddha*: Purity and Auspiciousness in Hindu
          Thought'. Paper presented to the Conference on Religion in South
          Asia, Washington, D.C.
Marglin, F.
  1981   'Kings and Wives: The Separation of Royal Status and Power',
          Contributions to Indian Sociology, n.s. (in press).
Marriott, McKim
  1968   'Caste Ranking and Food Transactions: A Matrix Analysis', in
          Structure and Change in Indian Society, ed. M. Singer & B. Cohn.
          Chicago: Aldine, 133–71.
  1973   'Hindu Transactions: Diversity Without Dualism'. Paper presented
          to the Symposium on *Transactional Analysis*. Oxford: ASA.
Mayer, Adrian C.
  1960   *Caste and Kinship in Central India: A Village and its Region.*
          Berkeley: University of California Press.
Mehta, R. N.
  n.d.   'Nagarkhanda' (MS.).

Misra, S. C.
  1962   *The Rise of Muslim Power in Gujarat*. Bombay: Asia Publishing
          House.

Munshi, K. M.
  1955   *Glory that was Gurjardesha*, vol. 2 Bombay: Bharatiya Vidya
          Bhavan.

Oldenberg, H.
  1892   *The Grihya Sutras*. Oxford: OUP.

Orenstein, Henry
  1968   'Toward a Grammar of Defilement in Hindu Sacred Law', in
          Structure and Change in Indian Society, ed. M. Singer & B. Cohn.
          Chicago: Aldine, 115–31.

Panikkar, K. M.
  1955   *Hindu Society at Crossroads*. Bombay: Popular Book Depot.

Pathak, Prabhashankar Jayshankar
  1924   *Dharmaranya Purana: Modh Jnatinu Pavitra Itihas*. Baroda: Modh
          Martanda (Sanskrit original with Gujarati trans.).

Pocock, David
  1962   'Notes on Jajmani Relations', *Contributions to Indian Sociology*, 6,
          78–95.
  1964   'The Anthropology of Time-Reckoning', *Contributions to Indian
          Sociology*, 7, 18–29.

Radcliffe-Brown, A. R.
  1933   'Social Conditions', *Encyclopaedia of the Social Sciences*. New
          York: Macmillan.

Raghavan, V.
  1960   'Tamil Versions of the Puranas', *Purana*, vol. 2. Varanasi: Kashiraj
          Trust.

Rawls, John
  1972   *A Theory of Justice*. Oxford: OUP.

Rigby, Peter
  1968   'Some Gogo Rituals of "Purification": An Essay on Social and
          Moral Categories', in *Dialectic in Practical Religion*, ed. E. Leach.
          Cambridge: CUP, 153–78.

Rommetveit, Ragnar
  1974   *On Message Structure: A Framework for the Study of Language and
          Communication*. London: John Wiley & Sons.

Sandesara, B. J. & R. N. Mehta (eds.)
  1964   *Mallapurana*. Baroda: Oriental Institute.

Sankarayanan, S.
  1968   *The Glory of the Divine Mother*. Madras.

Sarkar, S. C.
  1958   *Pauranik Abhidhan* (in Bengali). Calcutta: S. C. Sarkar & Sons
          Ltd.

Schneider, David
  1968   *American Kinship*: A Cultural Account. Englewood: Prentice-Hall.

Schweitzer, Albert
  1951   *Indian Thought and its Development*. London: H. Holt & Co.

Shah, A. M.
1973   *The Household Dimension of the Family in India.* Berkeley: University of California Press.
1976   'Lineage Structure and Change in a Gujarat Village', in *Dimensions of Social Change in India*, ed. M. N. Srinivas. New Delhi: Allied Publishers.

Shah, A. M. & Ramesh Shroff
1959   'The Vahivanca Barots of Gujarat: A Caste of Genealogists and Mythographers', in *Traditional India: Structure and Change*, ed. M. Singer. Philadelphia: American Folklore Society, 40–70.

Sharma, K. P.
1975   'A Note on the Word *Varna*', *Contributions to Indian Sociology*, n.s. 9, 293–7.

Srinivas, M. N.
1952   *Religion and Society Among the Coorgs of South India.* Oxford: OUP.
1962a   'Varna and Caste', in *Caste in Modern India and Other Essays.* Bombay: Asia Publishing House, 63–9.
1962b   'Village Studies and their Significance', in *Caste in Modern India and Other Essays.* Bombay: Asia Publishing House, 120–35.

Srinivas, M. N. & A. M. Shah
1968   'Hinduism', in *International Encyclopaedia of the Social Sciences*, ed. D. Sills. New York: Macmillan and The Free Press.

Stanner, W. E. H.
1959–63 'The Design Plan of a Riteless Myth', in *On Aboriginal Religion*, Oceania Monograph 2 (reprint of articles published in *Oceania* from Dec. 1959 – Sept. 1963).
1967   'Reflections on Durkheim and Aboriginal Religion', in *Essays on Social Organization*, ed. M. Freedman. London: Frank Cass & Co. Ltd., 217–40.

Stevenson, S.
1971   *The Rites of the Twice-Born.* New Delhi: Oriental Books Reprint Corporation (first published in 1920).

Tambiah, S.
1970   *Buddhism and the Spirit Cults in North-East Thailand.* Cambridge: CUP.
1976   *World Conqueror and World Renouncer.* Cambridge: CUP.

Thapar, Romila
1972   *A History of India, I.* Harmondsworth: Penguin.
1975   *The Past and Prejudice.* Delhi: National Book Trust.

Turner, Victor W.
1966   'Color Classification in Ndembu Ritual', in *Anthropological Approaches to the Study of Religion*, ed. M. Banton. London: Tavistock, 47–84.
1969   *The Ritual Process: Structure and Anti-structure.* London: Routledge & Kegan Paul.

Uberoi, J. P. S.
1967   'On Being Unshorn', in *Transactions of the Indian Institute of Advanced Study*, 4, 87–100.

van der Veen, Klass
  1972   *I Give Thee my Daughter*. Assen: Royal Van Gorcum.
van Gennep, Arnold
  1960   *The Rites of Passage* (trans. Monika B. Vizedom & G. L. Caffee).
           London: Routledge & Kegan Paul.
Wach, Joachim
  1944   *Sociology of Religion*. Chicago: University of Chicago Press.
Wadley, Susan
  1980   'Sitala: The Cool One', Asian Folklore Studies, vol. 39, 33–62.
Weber, Max
  1920–1   *Hinduismus und Buddhismus* (trans. H. Gerth & D. Martindale as
           The Religion of India). Glencoe: The Free Press, Tubingen.
Whitehead, Alfred N.
  1958   *Symbolism: Its Meaning and Effect*. London: Macmillan.

Author Index

Subject Index

Ancestors, 33, 63, 93-102, 105-11, 113, 119-20, 122, 124, 130, 144, 145, 146, 147, 149
Anuloma, 71. *See also* marriage
Ascetic, 29, 47, 123, 126, 129, 131, 138; asceticism, 7, 8, 46, 150. *See also* renouncer, *sanyasa, sanyasi*
Ashrama, 19, 34-6, 54, 86, 90
Asocial, 7, 38-9, 45-7
Auspicious, 140, 143n, 148
Auspicious and inauspicious, 128, 140, 143, 144, in relation to pure and impure, 128, 143, 145-7, 148
Brahmans, 6, 7, 9, 86-7, 89, 99, 130, 131, 133, 134, 135, 136, 137, 138, 139, 150, 151, 152; as mediators, 42, 44-51, 67, 110; characteristics of, 32-3, 34; creation of, 19, 31-2; dharma of, 32-4, 49, 62-4, 71-3; divisions among, 11, 57-62, 65-8, 79-82; in relation to impurity, 128-9; in relation to king and *sanyasi*, 28, 41-5, 47, 49, 53-4, 57, 67-9, 82, 131, 132, 134, 140, 148-9, 150, 151; in relation to *kshapanakas* 52-3; in relation to *sanyasi*, 40-1; in the conceptual order of Hinduism, 89; in Grihya Sutras, 99; life-style of, 110; relation between king and, 41-2, 46-9, 53-5, 66, 81, 86
Cardinal points, 9, 91, 104, 108; East, 104-5; North, 105; West, 105-6; South, 106
Caste, 1, 8, 9, 11-12, 51, 54, 55, 61, 164-5, 68-70, 74-7, 82, 85, 87, 109, 111, 113, 128-9, 142, 146, 154. *See also jati & varna*
Caste Puranas. *See* Puranas
Civilization, 5
Code of conduct, 62, 134
Commensal relations, 76
Corpse, 121, 122, 124, 146, 150. *See also* dead body
Cosmic, 9, 120, 125, 126

Cosmization, 129
Cremation, 8, 37, 94, 119, 121-3, 146, 150
Cult-group, 57, 70, 71, 82, 83, 84,
Dead body, 121-3
Death, 8, 50, 91, 98, 100, 102, 107, 111, 113, 119, 120-1, 123-5, 135, 136, 143, 144, 145, 146, 148, 150
Death rituals, 119, 120-6, 128-9, 141, 144, 145, 146, 149, 154
Descent, 57, 70, 71, 82, 83, 84, 101
Domestic ritual, 8, 91-3, 140, 142, 152
Endogamy, 34, 71, 73, 74, 82
Exchange, as a relation, 7; between Brahman and king, 42, 48-9, 66-7; language of, 57; of food, women, and ritual services, 57, 72-9, 152
Food, 63, 72, 74-9, 135, 137, 139. *See also* exchange of food, women, ritual services
Gift, 13, 23, 25, 49, 58, 62, 66, 78, 102, 135, 137, 139, 149, 150, 151
God, 23, 40, 99-102, 112, 113, 147, 148
Goddess, 24, 61-3, 103, 147, 148
Grihastha, 30, 33-7, 44, 53, 54. *See also* householder
Grihya sutras, 8, 17, 42, 93
Hierarchy, 51, 68-9, 73, 75-6, 82-3, 90, 141
Hinduism, 7-9, 15, 51, 54-6, 132, 140; conceptual order of, 57, 67-71, 82, 86-90, 132; Sanskritic and non-Sanskritic, 5, 8, 109-11, 113
Householder, 7, 33-4, 136, 137, 138, 139, 144, 149, 151
Human body, 9, 10, 81, 92, 126-8, 141, 142, 143, 144, 145
Hypergamy, 73-4, 77-8
Hypogamy, 73-4, 79
Impurity, 113, 119-31, 140, 142, 145, 146, 147, 148, 154. *See also* pollution, pure and impure
Inauspicious, 135, 144, 145